Literature-Based Moral Education

Literature-Based Moral Education

Children's Books & Activities for
Teaching Values, Responsibility, & Good Judgment
in the Elementary School

by Linda Leonard Lamme & Suzanne Lowell Krogh
with Kathy A. Yachmetz

Oryx Press
1992

The rare Arabian Oryx is believed to have inspired the myth of the unicorn. This desert antelope became virtually extinct in the early 1960s. At that time several groups of international conservationists arranged to have 9 animals sent to the Phoenix Zoo to be the nucleus of a captive breeding herd. Today the Oryx population is nearly 800, and over 400 have been returned to reserves in the Middle East.

Copyright © 1992 by Linda Leonard Lamme and Suzanne Lowell Krogh
Published by The Oryx Press
4041 North Central at Indian School Road
Phoenix, Arizona 85012-3397

Published simultaneously in Canada

Printed and Bound in the United States of America

∞ The paper used in this publication meets the minimum requirements of American National Standard for Information Science—Permanence of Paper for Printed Library Materials, ANSI Z39.48, 1984.

Library of Congress Cataloging-in-Publication Data
Lamme, Linda Leonard.
    Literature-based moral education: children's books and activities
for teaching values, responsibility, and good judgment in the
elementary school / by Linda Leonard Lamme and Suzanne Lowell Krogh
with Kathy A. Yachmetz.
        p. cm.
    Includes bibliographical references and index.
    ISBN 0-89774-723-2
    1. Moral education—United States.   2. Children—United States-
-Books and reading.   3. Activity programs in education—United
States.   I. Krogh, Suzanne.   II. Yachmetz, Kathy A.   III. Title.
LC311.L36   1992
370.11'4'0973—dc20   92-3190
                                                        CIP

Contents

Introduction:
A Book Is Born

SUZANNE

The child was unrepentant and the kindergarten teacher (Suzanne Krogh) was exasperated. She tried a new line of questioning.

"Do you know how Sam felt when you socked him?"

"No."

"Don't you remember what it felt like when you got hit on the jungle gym yesterday? Don't you think Sam felt the same way?"

"I dunno."

"Do you think Sam liked it when you hit him?"

"Maybe."

"Do you think it felt *good*?"

"Yes . . . no . . . I dunno."

Moving from frustration to anger, the teacher decided to stop the questioning altogether. Suzanne no longer recalls what happened next, but she does remember what she learned a year later from William Damon's newly published book, *The Social World of the Child* (1977): young children are unable to put themselves in someone else's shoes, socially or morally, until they are well into elementary school. Suddenly, the frustrating encounter of the year before came back to her and she realized that the unrepentant little boy really *didn't* know what Sam felt like. Chagrin at her earlier impatience and fascination with the newly developing field of early moral development and education led Suzanne to study further. Although young children may not reason about moral issues in the ways adults do, Suzanne was relieved and happy to discover that they can still be successfully encouraged to make sound moral decisions. Suzanne learned from her research that children are receptive to new ways of learning about moral issues, that they think about the issues very seriously, and that they find learning enjoyable.

As a doctoral student, Suzanne coauthored a book based on her research (Schuncke and Krogh, 1983), and later joined with another colleague to study the use of literature to promote moral development (Krogh and Lamme, 1985).

LINDA

At approximately the same time, a sixth grade teacher (Linda Lamme) inherited a classroom with basal readers that virtually none of the children in her class could hope to read. She escorted her students to the public library (there was no school library) five blocks away, every Friday morning. There the children learned how enjoyable and informative it can be to read real books and to publish a school newspaper. Her interest in literature continued to grow, spurred by a question from an uncle who was an avid reader. "What is it that schools do," he asked, "that makes some people who can read never touch a book, while other people like me would not be caught without a book?" (When Uncle Ed would visit Kucai, an island in the Pacific, accessible only once a month or so by medical ship, he would ship a crate of books ahead of him.) Linda's investigation into that question led her to explore the study of children's literature, and eventually, as a university professor, to embrace the whole language movement.

Most recently, Linda's academic preparation came alive when she was hired as a whole language consultant at Blackburn Elementary School in Manatee County, Florida. Watching that school's faculty move from a basic skills to a whole language curriculum in a very short time was inspiring beyond belief. It was from Blackburn's guidance counselor that she learned a lot about classroom management and prosocial development.

KATHY

In the spring of 1989 the guidance counselor at Blackburn Elementary (Kathy Yachmetz) completed a behavior management session with four second grade boys. Two boys earned a sticker for making a certain number of points on a behavior contract. Neither the boys nor Kathy could explain *why* the boys had earned these points from their teacher. Two boys did not earn enough points on their contract for a reward. They were resentful and angry. They had tried to be "good" but their definition of good was very vague. Frustrated by this process, Kathy gave the boys their new contracts for the upcoming week and sent them back to class. "This is not teaching them any responsibility," she thought, "only what behavior will pay off if the teacher is present." But what else was there to do in a school where the majority of teachers used behavior modification as their classroom discipline plan?

The following fall Blackburn hired a consultant to facilitate the school's move toward an integrated curriculum (whole language). "This doesn't really concern me," Kathy thought, "but I'll attend one of the in-service sessions to see what this whole language stuff is all about." Linda asked Kathy if she used children's books in the guidance program. She responded that she rarely did. She used mostly worksheets and games, or had the children do projects. Linda then gave Kathy an article on how a person can promote socio-emotional development in children by using literature (Jalongo, 1983).

Linda continued to facilitate Kathy's move to a literature-based guidance program, but that was not enough for Blackburn. The principal had asked for help in classroom management and discipline as a part of the in-service program, and what evolved from several sessions was the need for a positive, proactive, developmental discipline plan to coincide with the constructivist whole language philosophy. Kathy got excited and started working with teachers in their classrooms to teach children how to behave well—to solve conflicts peacefully, to listen to each other and the teacher, and to make friends—using children's literature as a basis of the program.

Now, two years after she attended that whole language session just to see what it was all about, Kathy has become the hands-on expert in facilitating children's moral development through her school's classroom management plan; Linda continues to teach children's literature and promote its use in classrooms; and Suzanne continues to write about moral education.

COLLABORATION

When the opportunity to write this book was presented to us, our three-way collaboration seemed ideal. We are three educators who believe that it is the responsibility of teachers, librarians, and parents to do something to guide children into becoming responsible members of society. Our own experiences have documented the growth that children can make through a teacher's efforts and we are hopeful about the possible success of others.

ABOUT OUR BOOK

In the first chapter, you will be brought up-to-date on what is now known about children's social/moral development and the implications for teaching. The second chapter presents similar information about children's literature and ways of generating responses to literature. The third chapter details strategies for using children's literature as a basis for moral education. The majority of the book is practical, presenting issues in moral development, children's books that deal with each of the issues, and ideas for classroom, library, or even home use. While it is possible to use this book by simply referring to the issues and choosing stories and activities, we hope that you will first take the time to read the introductory chapters. Not only will the practical ideas make more sense to you, but you will have a better idea of ways to invent your own activities for books that you discover on your own.

We are writing for any adults who work with children—parents, teachers, librarians, and counselors. However, because all three of us have backgrounds in education and practical classroom experience, most of our examples come from the classroom. The same strategies for sharing books with children can, however, be adapted easily to home, library, or counseling situations.

Most of the books we are recommending for use are picture books which normally would be associated with young children. We emphasize picture books because they are typically short enough to share in a short period of time with a child or group of children, and therefore are perfect for stimulating discussion or other responses. Most picture books with moral issues are suitable for older as well as younger children. Some have even been best-sellers among adults (*Oh, The Places You'll Go* and *Love You Forever*, for example). Because a book is a picture book does not mean that it is written exclusively for young audiences. Of course, chapter books can be the core of a moral education curriculum as well, and we have included a few reviews of longer books written expressly for older children. These, however, take longer to read and therefore would not provide as many opportunities over a period of time for reflection upon moral issues. In our reviews we have noted grade level designations for each book. These are our best estimates of the ages where the books might be most valuable. The designation "P" represents primary grades—kindergarten through grade 3. "I" represents intermediate—grades 3-5. You should feel free, however, to try any book at the age you think it might work. Books for older children often work nicely with younger ones, if they are read on a lap by a parent. Classroom readings are a bit more restricted.

Many of the books we have included have several moral issues in them and might fit well into several chapters of this book. Generally, when this arose, we placed the book into the chapter relating to its central moral issue. Several books, however, contained more than one equally strong moral issue and in those cases the books have been reviewed more than one time. Each review is very different, however, because a different aspect of the book is emphasized and the extension activities are different.

The books reviewed in these chapters are examples of the fine literature that is available for children today. It is our hope that these reviews will lead you to bookstores where you will find many others appropriate for your moral education curriculum. Using the ones we have reviewed as examples or models of the kinds of books that are available, you will be able to discover many more on your own. Similarly, the strategies we suggest for involving children in thoughtful considerations of the moral issues in the books are very open ended. It is our hope that we have provided enough examples and ideas for you to generate many more on your own. The key is adapting the general strategies to the book you are sharing so that you appropriately help children deal with the moral aspect of that book.

In other words, we hope that this book provides a springboard for adults to enjoyably engage children with literature containing important moral values. From these interactions, there is abundant evidence that children will mature in their moral development, becoming more capable, and feeling more worthwhile and needed by their families and friends.

REFERENCES

Damon, William. (1977). *The social world of the child.* San Francisco: Jossey-Bass.

Jalongo, M. R. (1983). Bibliotherapy: Literature to promote socioemotional growth. *The reading teacher.* 36, 8 (April): 796-803.

Krogh, Suzanne L. & Lamme, Linda L. (1985). Children's literature and moral development. *Young children.* 40, No. 4 (May): 48-51.

Schuncke, George & Krogh, Suzanne L. (1983). *Helping children choose.* Glenview, IL: Scott Foresman.

CHAPTER 1

What Are They Really Thinking?
Children and Moral Development

From earliest recorded times, and probably before then, adults have worried about and worked toward the moral development of their children. It was not until this century, however, that anyone made a systematic attempt at finding out what children are thinking when their parents and teachers exhort them to "be good"; or whether they actually understand goodness in the same way that adults do. The results of the first studies were surprising enough to turn centuries of moral training upside down.

PIAGET'S THEORIES

The researcher responsible for getting children to speak for themselves, after thousands of years of adult-only talk, was Jean Piaget, a Swiss biologist and psychologist. Piaget's research in the field of cognitive development is well known and is the focus of most of his life study. In addition, a single, but major research project in the 1920s led him (Piaget, 1932/1965) to draw some basic conclusions about children's moral development.

To get inside the minds of children, Piaget played with them (marbles and hopscotch, for example) and interviewed them. He discovered that the younger children are, the less likely they are to see goodness in thought and behavior in the same way adults do. In fact, his research led him to conclude that children grow in their understanding of morality in rather predictable stages.

Children below the ages of six or seven, Piaget found, can be designated as heteronomous. That is, they're not in the least autonomous, able to make knowledgeable moral decisions on their own. Rather, they look to authority figures to tell them what is right and what is wrong. On the positive side, this is the time of life when parents and teachers are most easily able to mold appropriate behavior. However, very young children also tend to behave as adults want them to only when it is in their self-interest: when they are rewarded with praise or food or toys, and when they can avoid punishment. They haven't yet internalized the reasons behind what others tell them is right to do.

Piaget also found an important cognitive element in children's moral understanding. He observed that children cannot reason about moral issues in a way that goes beyond their current intellectual stage. One of Piaget's interviews with children demonstrates how this is so with children who are still heteronomous.

In the interview, Piaget showed children pictures of a little girl who is happily helping her mother by carrying a tray full of china cups to the kitchen. The child accidentally stumbles, dropping the tray and breaking most of the cups. In a second set of pictures, the same little girl again carries the tray and stumbles, but this time the girl has a mean look on her face, stumbles on purpose, and there are only a few cups. Piaget asked children which situation called for stronger punishment. Children younger than six or seven were unable to focus on the good or bad intentions of the girl but were sidetracked by counting the broken cups. Their conclusion: if you break more cups you get more punishment.

Heteronomous children also have little understanding of rules. Preschool children playing football or baseball tend to focus on the fun "costumes" they get to wear and the opportunity to tear around the yard with a ball.

This is not true of children who are moving into the second stage, a transitional one between heteronomy and autonomy. Children in the primary grades latch onto rules as if they have found a new religion. This does not mean they always follow them of course, particularly when the rules conflict with their self-interest. But they perceive rules as being laws, laws that cannot ever be changed and that have been created by higher authorities: parents, teachers, even God. Considering their high regard for rules, it is not surprising that children of this age may almost obsessively tattle when they believe someone has broken the rules.

In this transitional stage, children who see the two sets of Piaget pictures are not thrown by the numbers of broken cups. They now understand that intentions are important. In a playground dispute, the accusation, "He hit me on purpose!" will carry more weight and have more meaning.

Still, children are far from being autonomous. Because they can't put themselves in the shoes of the people who make the rules and laws they have only a one-sided view of them. They know they had better follow the rules or they'll be in some kind of trouble, and they sometimes see themselves as following the rules even when they aren't.

Children are 11 or 12 before they are capable of real autonomy. This kind of thinking requires that they be able to see rules, laws, and social or moral situations from other people's perspectives. It even demands that they be able to step completely outside a complex social situation and see the many and varied viewpoints within it. As we all know, this is sometimes difficult even for adults!

At the autonomous stage, children understand that rules were made by human beings like themselves and that they can therefore be changed if appropriate. Are there only a few kids available to play ball? The goalposts can be placed closer together or there can be just two bases instead of three.

KOHLBERG'S THEORY

Piaget did not continue his seminal research in the field of moral development, but focused his energies on the study of cognition. It was not until the 1960s that someone took up the challenge to delve further into children's moral thought. An America psychologist, Lawrence Kohlberg, became the first to expand upon Piaget's original study.

Kohlberg's earliest studies looked at boys between the ages of 10 and 16. He interviewed them in the style of Piaget and ultimately created a stage theory that takes people from early childhood through the most sophisticated levels of adult thought. At the earlier stages, those pertaining to this book, Kohlberg relied on Piaget's study, so we need not discuss his work further. However, Kohlberg's research is important because it led Moshe Blatt, one of Kohlberg's graduate students, to carry out a further study that altered Kohlberg's own thinking about development. In fact, without Blatt's study this book would never have been written.

Kohlberg was a psychologist, interested in the way children develop but detached from their moral education, believing that it would make little difference in development. Blatt, however, believed that education could make a difference. He expanded on the Piaget/Kohlberg interview style, trying something similar with school children in discussion groups. After analyzing pretests and posttests, Blatt found that such discussions could help children make statistically significant gains in their moral development stages. Since that remarkable discovery, a number of other researchers and educators have been looking at ways to enhance children's moral understanding. This book is a product of such research and work in classrooms.

DAMON'S WORK

Other researchers in psychology have continued studying the development of younger children, describing more fully the heteronomous, transitional, and autonomous stages that Piaget discovered. One of these researchers, William Damon, has looked at such early childhood moral and social issues as friendship, relationships to authority, and positive justice (distribution of available goods). The last of these provides a good example of the ways in which Piaget's theory can be expanded into very specific areas of development.

At the early childhood and elementary level, positive justice can best be described as sharing. To study the development of understanding about sharing, Damon interviewed children, in the Piaget tradition, by telling an open-ended story. It takes place in a school classroom where the children all make pictures which are later sold at the weekend school fair. The following Monday, the teacher asks the children who should get the profits. The story ends here and a series of questions about what should happen next provide the interviewer with a good overall picture of the interviewee's understanding of positive justice. Here are the levels of development Damon observed with some answers an interviewer might expect to hear at each of them. The ages are approximate.

- **Level 0-A (ages 3-4).** Choices are based on the child's egocentric wishes. "I should get all the money. I like money!"
- **Level 0-B (ages 3-5).** Choices are based on the child's own desires justified by external, physical qualities. "The kids should get some money but the teacher's got to have lots because she's biggest."
- **Level 1-A (ages 4-6).** Choices are based on a desire for strict equality. "Everybody should get exactly the same, no matter what!"
- **Level 1-B (ages 5-7).** Choices are made based on reciprocity and merit. Concern for the disadvantaged first appears. "The poor kids should get just a tiny bit more money, but only if they do some extra work first."
- **Level 2-A (ages 7-9).** Children believe that different persons can have equally valid justifications for their choices. "We'll give a little extra to the poor kids and a little extra to the ones that worked the hardest. Everybody else will get the same."
- **Level 2-B (ages 8-10).** Children can consider various claims and situational demands when making choices. "Usually I'd say that the kids who work the hardest should get the most money. But, in this case, they weren't really working. They painted and went to the fair because it was fun. Either everybody should get the same or they should donate the money to the school if it needs it."

Notice the theme of equality that pops up at different levels. Once an idea appears, as equality does at Level 1-A, it stays with the child, becoming a part of future considerations. Notice, too, how closely Damon's observations of children fit with Piaget's. Children of preschool age are concerned primarily with their own needs, as well they should be since they need to know themselves first and best before moving into the larger world. Their first foray into selflessness appears at Level 2-A when they begin to realize that there are people with special needs who may deserve extraordinary consideration.

SELMAN'S WORK

One final researcher rounds out our discussion of moral development studies. Robert Selman, using Piagetian interviews, has studied the development of children's perceptions of self and others. He, too, found the youngest children most focused on self and the older ones able to see most clearly that others have differing, and sometimes equally valid, points of view. Selman refers to this growth from egocentrism outward as the development of social perspective taking. This ability is more than a skill that makes social interactions more successful. There is a moral element to it that comes from our need to step into each other's shoes to understand how our actions toward others will be received. Selman studied children from preschool age through adolescence, and the stages he discovered look like this:

- **Stage 0 (ages 3-6).** Children are at their most egocentric and can't distinguish between their own social perspectives and others' perspectives. They can recognize someone else's overt behaviors and respond to them from their own perspective: "Daddy looks sad. Maybe I'd better let him hold my blanket." (The younger child may even expect Daddy to suck his thumb while holding the treasured blanket.)
- **Stage 1 (ages 6-8).** Children are aware that others may have different perspectives and can respect the validity of those perspectives. But they can focus on just one viewpoint at a time, unaware that situations may be more complex. When pushed, they will prefer their own perspective to another's: "If I take the last piece of candy, my sister won't get as many as I did. But red's my favorite, so she won't care."
- **Stage 2 (ages 8-10).** Children have a better understanding that people can have varying viewpoints and are beginning to understand that they can have mixed feelings about a situation themselves. They see these feelings as sequential rather than truly mixed, however, sometimes

thinking of different feelings as assigned to different parts of the brain: "Sure, sometimes I have mixed feelings about being happy and sad. First I'm happy, then I'm sad, then I'm happy . . . "

* **Stage 3 (ages 10-12)**. Children are able to step outside a social situation and view its complexities. They know that people's feelings about a single situation can be complex and that they aren't always completely aware of their own feelings: "You know, I was feeling sad and didn't even know it until you asked me why I looked so gloomy."

TRANSLATING THEORIES INTO PRACTICE

One major reason for the similarities between Piaget's, Damon's, and Selman's observations of children is that they observed similar types of development across almost identical ages. A second reason is that all three come from a similar philosophical and theoretical view. The theories derived from this shared viewpoint have their beginnings in the studies done by Piaget and are often referred to under the umbrella term, *constructivism.* Constructivists see children responding to the environment; they also believe that a child's own biology is important. As children use what nature has given them to interact with what is supplied by the environment, they construct their own knowledge. Not all researchers of children's social/ moral development share this view. Some subscribe instead to the social learning theory which has children developing almost entirely in response to their social interactions with others, while others prefer the psychoana- lytic view with its roots in the work of Freud.

Even among constructivists and between researchers who subscribe in part to constructivist theory there are disagreements about child develop- ment. Some have found that children achieve the designated stages sooner than indicated by Piaget. Damon (1983), for example, states that further analyses of Piaget's own data reveal considerably more communicative exchange, even among his youngest subjects, than Piaget acknowledged. Damon suggests that contemporary research has shown that children as young as four can communicate nonegocentrically with each other.

Other new findings imply that there are some tasks within an area of understanding (such as sharing or perspective taking) that children can do with ease, and other tasks that prove more difficult. These findings are important for users of this book because they indicate that role-taking, the ability to take another's perspective, is possible for children at younger ages than was previously thought. It is children's ability to take the role of the central characters in books that primarily helps them understand the moral lessons involved in the story.

Other researchers argue against the kind of stage structure established by Damon and Selman. Damon himself finds some agreement with researchers who argue for broader categories of development. He suggests that role-taking development is continuous—that there are no stages: "Rather, developmental changes in perspective taking itself are more on the order of how often and how comprehensively the child considers the perspectives of others" (Damon, 1983, p. 126). Systematic and regular exposure to quality literature containing moral dilemmas, then, can help children at all stages internalize the reasoning behind developing empathy for others.

While such disagreements don't help teachers who try to make practical sense of developmental theory, they do provide some good news. Increasingly it has been found that children are capable of many moral behaviors and understandings at earlier ages than previously thought. Even four-year-olds can communicate nonegocentrically and begin to role-take, an important first step in developing morally.

Looking more closely at this critical ability to take on the role of another and develop empathy, Damon sees the need for a deeper analysis of this one aspect of moral development. The age-ranges of the stages in this aspect of social and moral development are broader than those for overall moral development. Two of the stages related to the ages represented in this book include:

- **Stage 2 (ages 2-6)**. First children can place themselves in the other's place and find the true source of the distress; and second, they can make an assessment of the other's needs. Children become more effective at both sensing and treating discomfort in their friends.
- **Stage 3 (ages 6-9)**. Children become concerned about the general condition of persons, rather than only about situationally caused distresses. Children are sensitive to the general plight of life's chronic victims—the poor, the handicapped, the socially outcast. This opens the way for a new domain of prosocial activity: the concerted effort to aid those less fortunate than oneself.

In our own experiences we have found that children who are in a literature-based reading program want to become activists even in the first grade. They have joined Greenpeace, adopted manatees, and expressed concern for the homeless. Second graders have prepared meals for a parent coming home from the hospital and started a schoolwide fund raiser for starving children in Ethiopia. Such caring behaviors, even if not fully understood by every child in the class, do give children increased opportunities to grow out of the more egocentric stages of moral development.

Earlier, we said that centuries of moral training had been turned upside down by the discoveries of the researchers you have just read about. Traditionally, adults have tried in various ways to pass their values on to the next generation. But, they haven't understood that children don't absorb the lessons in the same way they are given. As children construct their own intellects and their codes of moral ethics, they begin with very primitive structures, seeing the issues from their very limited experience. When an adult tells a child she or he must be "good," the child interprets that word according to her or his stage of development. If the adult then probes the child's reasoning about this admonition, the answers may be somewhat surprising.

In our own research with young children, this has often been the case. Once, Suzanne was interviewing a first grader about sharing issues, using Damon's picture selling story. The conversation between the interviewer (I) and the child (C) went something like this:

(I) So, who should get the money for the pictures?

(C) They should all share. (Sanctimoniously) It's good to share, you know.

(I) Really? Why is it good to share?

(C) Because my daddy says so and he's a preacher so he knows.

(I) Why do you think a preacher says it's good to share?

(C) 'Cuz Jesus told him to.

(I) Why do Jesus and a preacher both think it's good to share?

(C) 'Cuz God told them.

(I) Okay. Why do God and Jesus and a preacher all think it's good to share?

(C) I don't know. But if I don't share I know I'll get a whippin'.

Two things about this amusing interchange are quite typical. First, the interviewer continues to probe the child's reasoning to find the bottom line, the real underlying structure of the child's thinking. In this case, it took awhile to get beyond what the child thought he should say to what he really thought. Second, this conversation reveals that what the father thought he was passing on to his son about the importance of sharing was no more than a surface understanding of the adult view of sharing. The child, wanting to please his dad and avoid punishment, could say all the right words, but had no idea of the reasoning behind his behavior. While obedience is an important character trait for children, blind obedience makes the child rely totally on the adult for decision making and deprives the child of the autonomy needed to make further decisions on his or her own. Children must understand *why* there is a need to behave in morally and ethically sound ways.

Does this kind of interchange argue against adults trying to enhance children's moral growth? Not if we take the experience of Moshe Blatt and other subsequent researchers seriously. But it is important to remember, first, that children see moral issues in a way that is very different from our own; and, second, that the educational experiences we provide must give children the freedom to construct their own intellects and moral ethics based on their current stage of development.

Our society today is far less homogeneous than it has been in the past. One thing for certain is that you will have in your classroom children from more diverse social, ethnic, cultural, and economic backgrounds than ever before. Such diversity in home conditions creates children at much more diverse levels of moral development. We can no longer assume that the children in our school classes have a supportive and stimulating moral environment or average intellectual capabilities. That is why teachers are so important in the moral development process. If children don't learn values in school, they may never learn them. On the other hand, some families today are more nurturing and well informed about child care and development than ever before in our history. Some of their children may have developed morally beyond what has been typical for their ages. Lickona (1983) suggests that the levels of moral development of Piaget, Kohlberg, and Damon are reasonable goals for a moral development curriculum. Most children with whom we work have a good chance of attaining each particular stage.

Since you will have children at differing stages of development in your classroom, and since children are never completely stable in their stages but are constantly growing, it is impossible for you to be completely aware of where they are when you teach them. However, the theories we have just described give approximate ages which will give you good general guidelines for discussions, activities, and the books you choose. As an example, you may want to read *Something to Crow About* (Lane, 1990, discussed in Chapter 4) to your kindergarten class. This book shows ways in which children can focus on themselves and their glorious individuality. For children who are still in an egocentric stage this is entirely appropriate. Fourth graders, although they still need to feel good about themselves, should probably devote more time to books that help them take another's point of view. A good choice for them might be *The Big Book for PEACE* (Furrell & Sachs, 1990, see Chapter 8) or *The Christmas Coat* (Bulla, 1990, see Chapter 8).

In summary, it seems clear that children respond to moral issues at whatever levels of development coincide with their abilities to reason. We need to be sensitive to these levels of development when selecting books and developmentally appropriate activities for children. Because there is a great deal of diversity within classrooms, we need to provide open-ended response opportunities so that children at all levels of development are challenged to grow morally. Adults (parents, librarians, and teachers) are often more inclined to lecture at children or guide them directly by pointing out moral behavior. Children grow more and internalize their moral beliefs when they have opportunities to reason and think things through at their own level. We adults must stifle our efforts to preach about morals and instead learn to facilitate children's own thinking about these issues. Finally, the amount and quality of children's exposure to the views and behaviors of others, which literature so richly provides, can have a lasting impact on children's moral development.

The stories we have chosen for classroom use and the activities that accompany them have been carefully selected for stage appropriateness. Nevertheless, you will need to make further judgments based upon the needs of your own children. The children interviewed by Piaget, Damon, Selman, and their associates came from all walks of life and from varying cultures. While the researchers found that the progression of developmental stages seemed to be the same everywhere, children in different cultures achieved the stages at different ages. The way your students reason and behave and the progress they make will depend to some extent on their own backgrounds. Now that you have made your way through this rather theoretical chapter, you will also be able to choose books and activities that suit your children's stages and encourage your children to construct their own sense of right and wrong.

The following chapter will give you more ideas for selecting quality literature. For books to have maximum impact upon children's moral development they not only need to contain stage-appropriate moral dilemmas, but also be examples of the best in children's literature. Even if there is a very appropriate moral dilemma, if children don't relate to that problem and are not enticed into reading the book, the situation will have no impact.

REFERENCES

Damon, William. (1977). *The social world of the child.* San Francisco: Jossey-Bass.

————. (1983). *Social and personality development.* New York: W. W. Norton.

Kohlberg, Lawrence. (1976). Moral stages and moralizations: The cognitive-developmental approach. In Thomas Lickona (Ed.), *Moral development and behavior.* New York: Holt, Rinehart & Winston.

Lickona, Thomas. (1983). *Raising good children: Helping your child through the stages of moral development.* Toronto: Bantam.

Piaget, Jean. (1932, 1965). *The moral judgment of the child.* New York: Macmillan.

Selman, Robert. (1976). Social-cognitive understanding: A guide to educational and clinical practice. In Thomas Lickona (Ed.), *Moral development and behavior.* New York: Holt, Rinehart & Winston.

CHAPTER 2

Why Literature? A Rationale

There are many approaches to promoting moral development in children. In her book on creative ways to promote social and moral development, Carolyn Pope Edwards (1986) shares thinking games, discussions with children, and a variety of classroom activities. At the end of each chapter she lists children's books which are chosen to depict the positive images or attitudes discussed in the chapter. This would suggest that Edwards views books as models of appropriate social and moral behavior. Because children's literature often presents traditional roles and experiences, Edwards points out the importance of balancing children's literary diets so as to expose the children to cultures, experiences, and attitudes different from their own.

Literature provides a natural resource for parents, teachers, and librarians to share with children in ways that enhance their moral development. Field and Weiss (1987) provide reviews of several hundred books for children and young adults centering around 10 values: cooperation, courage, friendship and love of animals, friendship and love of people, humaneness, ingenuity, loyalty, maturing, responsibility, and self-respect. The Field and Weiss book is an excellent guide to book selection on the topic of values.

Merely reading books including moral values is not enough. Children attend to many different things when reading or listening to a story. Some are entranced by the illustrations; others notice and relate to the characters; others may be reminded by the setting of experiences in their lives; and others are deeply involved in the plot. By building on children's natural inclinations to identify with different aspects of stories, a moral education curriculum can provide opportunities for considering the moral dimension of stories. Thoughtful discussion, writing, reflecting, and sharing of books can help children acquire more sophisticated aspects of moral behavior. This book shares literature which can promote moral development along with strategies for involving children in thoughtful reflection about the moral issues in the books.

LITERATURE AS A VIEW OF THE WORLD OUTSIDE SELF

Children, especially at younger ages, typically have a strong interest in themselves. As they mature, they learn to look outward to others in their family, their school, and the world. Children's literature plays an important function in introducing children to the world outside their immediate lives. It provides an important link between children's experiences and the experiences of others. As they hear how characters in books behave and why, children compare those actions to their own. They learn to place themselves in the role of the protagonist in stories and to predict how the protagonist might act or how they would act if they were in the story themselves.

Young children, being at the more egocentric stages of moral development, tend to view the world from their own perspectives and cannot see other points of view. The use of literature can be a nonthreatening way to help them begin to see things from other perspectives. As they identify with characters in stories, children learn role-taking, which can lead to the development of empathy and the ability to reason from more than an egocentric point of view. They move from developing empathy for story characters in a role-playing situation to developing empathy and kindness in real situations. Literature offers many opportunities to practice the kinds of behavior we would like to see children adopt in real life.

When they encounter thinking that is divergent from their own, children see that there are many different ways of looking at situations. They begin to value differences among people, become more tolerant individuals, and are better able to interact socially. Children feel better about themselves when they see where their viewpoints and lives fit in with the views and lifestyles of those living around them.

LITERATURE ABOUT MORAL ISSUES AND EXPERIENCES

Many children's books—nonfiction and poetry as well as fiction—contain moral dilemmas. Living ethically is a part of life and therefore appears as an issue in literature. Think back to some really good books you have read lately. Don't most of those books contain values and moral decisions? Fiction books use moral issues to help readers relate to the plot of the story and to make them empathize with the protagonist. A dull story is one that has a superficial plot and merely tells what is happening without much consideration for why events are occurring. Good contemporary nonfiction literature contains not only information, but discussion of attitudes about that information, and in some cases, ethical or unethical actions on the part of people who use that information. Nonfiction is one way authors help children become activists. And poetry is full of affective thoughts and feelings in language that is meant to move the reader. Taken in its totality, then, all forms of children's literature contain moral and ethical views and values.

Marian Pyles (1988) has compiled reviews of many children's books on the topic of death and dying. She found, while teaching a course in children's literature, that the theme of death was prevalent in children's stories. Using her own background as an expert on the topic of death and dying, she reviewed many books, both folklore and realistic fiction, on the death of a pet, the death of a friend, the death of a relative, and one's own death. The author's philosophy is that the ultimate answer to death is living and loving to the fullest. Most of the books reviewed are long chapter books suitable for older children. There are no strategies for teaching included in the Pyles book, but the author does speak out forcefully against techniques classified as bibliotherapy. She calls bibliotherapy an alarming trend in the field of children's literature, defining it as therapy through books. The use of books to help children resolve their emotional and psychological problems has resulted in the publication of many books containing inferior writing and illustration and heavy doses of didacticism. Didacticism simply does not work. "Bibliotherapy, in its emphasis on telling, not showing, sacrifices both art and meaning" (p. 11). Fortunately, Pyles is able to conclude that much children's literature deals tastefully, truthfully, and artistically with the subject of death.

We share the views of Pyles about bibliotherapy in its didactic sense. However, the term is not always defined in such a rigid manner. Some writers *share* literature with children (instead of "using" it) for the purpose of role playing, reflecting upon, and discussing issues raised by the story and children's life experiences. Such open-ended activities, when they focus upon quality literature, can be very therapeutic without being didactic. Literature in the moral development curriculum is also bibliotherapeutic in nature, but from a preventative standpoint. In other words, children can read literature which can influence their lives before problems occur. Literature can provide strategies for dealing with moral dilemmas prior to and during children's encounters with these issues, and not only after they have taken place.

Rudman (1984) takes a much more kindly view of the term "bibliotherapy." She states that the use of books to help children solve their personal problems and become aware of societal concerns has become an accepted part of teaching. "In using bibliotherapy educators do not assume the role of psychologists or physicians, but recognize that children today walk into the classroom with their minds crowded with issues" (p. 3). Rudman cautions against being prescriptive or forced, and instead advocates regular reading aloud by the teacher and conferences between the teacher and child as approaches to expose children to books on moral education.

The issues presented by Rudman include the family, sex, gender roles, heritage, special needs, old age, death, and war. Although Rudman does suggest some activities, most of them are to develop sensitivity to the topic on the part of the reader instead of activities related to the children's books from her annotated bibliographies. The vast majority of the books reviewed by Rudman are chapter books for older children.

LITERATURE AS A MODEL

Sometimes it is hard to find models of moral behavior, especially child models to whom children can readily relate. You may have to wait all day for a real example of a child who solves a problem peacefully or someone who reaches out kindly to others. Literature provides many such models. In many children's books there are actions which reflect moral decision making and behavior. When children read about the behaviors of other people, they can relate those to their own lives and reflect upon their own behavior. Literature models can be very powerful; if you just talk with a child about a moral issue, there is nothing to refer back to when the discussion is over. We often tend to remind children or nag, rather than helping them learn to accept responsibility for their actions. Books allow us to refer back to the actions of a character. "Remember how David's sister behaved in *Dogger*?" gives the child a referent to turn to when making moral decisions. And because David's sister is a step removed from the child, referring to her is less threatening and sounds less like nagging.

Madeleine L'Engle writes in the introduction to *Triumphs of the Spirit in Children's Literature* (Butler & Rotert, 1986) about her granddaughter who spent a summer in hospitals after an accident which, by all rights, should have killed her. The first thing the child requested when she gained consciousness was to be read to. The family read until they were hoarse, relates L'Engle, and the child was healed, without any whining or self-pity. "She was healed by doctors and nurses, but also by the stories she heard that summer. Children in literature are glorious examples of the triumph of the human spirit, but they triumph in literature because they triumph in life. The children in the books we read to my granddaughter affirmed her own response to what had happened to her, and encouraged her own natural courage. Literature and life nourish each other" (p. xvii). L'Engle ends with a plea to give our children the very best so that they will be stretched creatively and spiritually. She obviously views books as very powerful resources for children's moral and spiritual development.

The examples of prosocial behavior in literature only serve as models when children view them that way. Sometimes that takes a specific curriculum designed to highlight a moral value and to help children reflect thoughtfully upon that value. A literature-based curriculum not only exposes children to a wide variety of excellent literature, it also provides for suitable extension activities which promote children's love of literature and raises the level at which they interact with what they are reading. Role playing, discussion, and sharing literature orally, in writing, and through projects all offer potential for thoughtful reflection about the moral values and issues in children's books.

RESPONSES TO LITERATURE

What do *you* do after you have read a book that you enjoyed? Are you given a test to determine what you learned (or comprehended) from the story? Do you fill out a worksheet or ditto asking you questions about the book? No. You share the book with someone you think might be interested in reading about it, or tell your friends about the book. The book might inspire you to take some action, to think about your life, or to handle a problem. These kinds of activities—discussion and activities related to the book—are called responses to literature. They differ dramatically from the testing approach.

In a testing mode, the teacher or adult asks children questions about what they read. The purpose is to determine if the children actually read what they were supposed to read, and if they comprehended the material. A response-oriented curriculum rarely asks children questions about what they read, but if it does, the questions seek the opinions of the reader and are asked because the adult is really interested in finding out how the child felt about the story. And, more interesting questions also answer the basic one: Did the child read and comprehend the book? June McConaghy (1990) discusses the dramatic change that took place in her teaching when she began conducting research in her first grade classroom about how children responded to children's literature. A key element in the new approach was her method of dealing with children after they had read a book. Her questions changed from testing whether children comprehended what they read to asking their opinions about the books. She really wanted to know how they felt about what they read and that orientation led to genuine discussions about books that were at a much higher level of response than she had achieved earlier when she was only concerned with how well the children were reading.

As teachers make the transition from a comprehension-based curriculum to a response-oriented curriculum, the nature of the questions they ask children changes from asking questions they already know the answers to (testing questions) to asking questions they want to find out the answers to (authentic questions). Three questions that have been useful to many teachers in making this transition are: (a) What did you notice in the story? (b) How did the story make you feel? (c) What does this story remind you of in your own life? (Kelly, 1990) From these prompting questions, children learn to conduct discussions independently of an adult, without the need for questions to focus their discussions about the books they are reading. Instead, they need time to talk about books.

Questions that we have found helpful in working with children include the following:

1. *What happened in the story?* This question focuses the children's attention on what actually happened and assures that they understood what they read.

2. *Why did this happen?* A key to understand the moral value in a story is understanding the characters' motives for behaving the way they do. This question helps children attribute meaning to the story.

3. *How did this make the story characters feel?* In order to move up the scale of moral development, children need to understand how other people feel and how one person's actions influence another's feelings.

4. *How did this make you feel?* In order to respond at a personal level, the children have to have both affective and cognitive responses to a story. Unless a story impacts their feelings, the moral lessons in it are likely to be lost.

5. *What does this remind you of in your own life?* For children to internalize any of the ethical themes, they must link them to their own life experiences.

6. *Did you learn something from reading this story?* What was it? This question can elicit more thoughtful reflection about the moral theme of a book.

Talking About Books (Short & Pierce, 1990) shares many strategies teachers use to help children talk intelligently about the books they are reading. In classrooms where teachers focus upon encouraging literate talk about literature, children and the teacher form learning communities that support readers as they read and interact with others. Often these interactions involve discussion of the moral issues presented in books. They lead children into deeper explorations within a book. "Literature provides children with a wide variety of characters and experiences of the past and present. As children weigh the truth of these stories in relationship to their own lives, they can begin to reflect on their values and place in society" (p. 12). Ralph Peterson and Maryann Eeds (1990) state that what we don't need is more children who are plot readers—children who just read through the text to find out what will happen to the characters. What we need is children who take an active role in reading, who relate what they are reading about to their own lives. Short and Pierce call this a transactional view of reading, in which each reader takes something different from the reading because each relates what is in the book to her or his own life experiences. A curriculum then, no longer simply imparts knowledge, but helps children enrich their personal experience through intelligent interaction with literature.

In schools and classrooms where whole language instruction is in practice, teachers work to generate high levels of response to literature with their children. Instead of teaching children reading skills or asking questions about reading comprehension, teachers encourage children to share the literature they read through oral and written responses. The idea is that if a child can respond to literature, that child has certainly comprehended it and used whatever skills were needed to understand what was written.

What constitutes a high level response to literature? One way to think about responses is to determine which ones will have the greatest impact upon a child's life. Responses which reflect actions and behaviors on the part of a child are higher level responses than are simple, direct answers to questions that adults ask at the end of a story. Responses that analyze why a story character behaved the way she or he did are higher than statements like, "I liked the story." Many of the kinds of responses that are generated by stories where children make moral decisions are high level responses to literature.

Peterson and Eeds outline important literary features that can become the focus of a response-oriented curriculum. Especially important to the moral education curriculum are responses that deal with the main character in the story and reasons for that character's behavior. Also worth noting are responses to plot, especially if the plot involves logical consequences for human behavior. Responses to mood in a story can help children go beyond just thinking about a story on a literal level, to analyzing the emotions involved and their own responses to those emotions. Such responses are more likely to lead to actions on the part of the reader, to changed moral thinking and behavior. Children become "crusaders in the classroom" when they are moved to action by something they have read.

The following chart highlights some of the characteristics of a child's low, moderate, and high level responses to literature:

High-level response (transactions with text)
> refers to tone and mood of the story
> refers to text and interprets it
> relates to emotions
> is child-initiated
> is detailed and planned
> is individual, imaginative, and not copied
> is multifaceted (artistic, musical, dramatic, written, and oral)
> explores reasons why authors have written the way they have

Moderately high response (analysis and synthesis)
> includes plot recognitions/theme/main idea
> is analytical: analyzes pictures or story
> includes references to other stories: book links
> includes genre generics/genre comparisons (synthesis)
> involves predictions vs story endings
> translates story to own experiences
> understands a particularly difficult, but important aspect of the book
> > (*example:* recognizes it is a dream)
> refers to the literature in later conversations
> is collaborative
> seeks out more information on a topic or about an author

Moderate response (role-playing)
> gives reasons for liking the book
> retells the story
> quotes the text to respond to questioning
> takes a character's role in the story

Low response (literal)
> "I like the book."
> "It was good."
> memorizes all or part of the story word for word
> has literal recall of the story
> answers factual questions about the story with one right answer

In our experiences with children we have concluded that a small group discussion generally results in higher levels of response than a large group. Responses are higher when children can actually hold the book in their hands. Responses are higher when the teacher is a part of a group rather than when the teacher leads a discussion or sits on the sidelines while the children work independently. Responses are higher when children give opinions and have discussions than when they just answer teacher questions.

Responses to literature can vary depending upon the types of books children are reading. Every kind of literature offers contributions to the moral education curriculum. When reading nonfiction, children tend to seek out more information, to organize in some way (charts, graphs, maps, etc.) what they are learning, to record what they are learning and their personal responses to that information, and to use the information they read about.

Folk literature is full of information about the culture from which the tale comes. This information includes the attitudes and habits of that culture. As children retell and create their own stories, they thoughtfully entertain the moral values. Folk literature is full of good triumphing over bad with clear distinctions between good and bad characters and actions. Some folk literature, like fables, has clearly stated morals, while other types of folk literature are more subtle in their presentation of values.

Realistic fiction allows children to relate story plots to their own life experiences and to develop empathy for story characters. Children use fiction literature as a model for their own behavioral choices. Similarly, biography and autobiography are very reflective kinds of literature that lend insight into people and into the reasons why those individuals behaved the way they did. These kinds of literature help children focus on the lives of people and upon their own lives to determine the ethical nature of their life choices.

In Masha Rudmon's *Children's Literature: An Issues Approach* (1984), Jane Yolen comments about how children's responses to literature differ from those of adults. Adults read something and react to it. They either accept it or reject it. The same is not true for children. "A child reader reads with the heart. And so, if I write for children, I must be aware that children are going to accept what I write with their hearts. My morality becomes their morality. Heart to heart, body to body, blood to blood, a kind of literary eucharist" (p. xi). This kind of intimacy between author and reader is the core of the literary experience.

Instead of outlining specific activities to be completed by children after reading a book, we will generate a number of potential responses or activities that would promote high level responses to the literature. Sharing these books will then benefit the literature curriculum as well as the moral education curriculum.

LITERATURE AND MORAL DEVELOPMENT

Two of the authors of this book (Suzanne Krogh and Linda Lamme, 1983 & 1985) have written about their experiences using literature with children in one area of moral education. They saw first-hand how adults can stimulate children's growth in moral reasoning by using children's literature as a basis for role playing and discussion. The other author of this book (Kathy Yachmetz) has spent two years working with classroom teachers to involve children with literature in ways that help the children become more caring and thoughtful of each other in the classroom. She has seen striking examples of how literature has helped individual children develop prosocial ways of behaving.

The following strategies for promoting thoughtful consideration of the moral issues in children's books appear throughout this book as they relate to the specific titles we review.

- Creating a story web of ideas for further interaction with a book, and, in particular, determining how the book relates to the children's lives.
- Brainstorming with a group of children the possible choices or decisions a story character might make.
- Writing or discussing how we would behave in situations similar to those a story character faces.
- Writing or discussing how we feel about a character's decisions.
- Writing about or discussing experiences in our own lives that are similar to those the story characters face.
- Role playing a part of a story that involves choices in behaviors and exploring through role play the alternatives and their consequences.
- Graphing and charting characters' feelings at various places during the plot of the story.
- Drawing pictures to make more clear what is important in the stories being shared.

The value of literature in a moral education curriculum depends upon two things. First, the quality of the literature provided for children to read (and thus the quality and depth of values and issues presented in the literature) is vital. Second, the types of thoughtful engagements with literature that are offered by the curriculum and the environment in which the books are shared with children determine the impact of the literature upon children.

REFERENCES

Butler, Francelia & Rotert, Richard. (1986). *Triumphs of the spirit in children's literature.* Hamden, CT: Library Professional Publications.

Edwards, Carolyn Pope, with Ramsey, Patricia G. (1986). *Promoting social and moral development in young children: Creative approaches for the classroom.* New York: Teachers College Press.

Field, Carolyn W. & Weiss, Jacquiline Shachter. (1987). *Values in selected children's books of fiction and fantasy.* Hamden, CT: Library Professional Publications.

Kelly, Patricia R. (1990). Guiding young students' response to literature. *The reading teacher.* (March): 464-470.

Krogh, Suzanne L. & Lamme, Linda L. (1983). Learning to share: How literature can help. *Childhood education.* 59 (January/February): 188-192.

———. (1985). Children's literature and moral development. *Young children.* 40, No.4 (May): 48-51.

McConaghy, June. (1990). *Children learning through literature.* Portsmouth, NH: Heinemann.

Peterson, Ralph & Eeds, Maryann. (1990). *Grand conversations.* Toronto: Scholastic.

Pyles, Marian S. (1988). *Death and dying in children's and young people's literature: A survey and bibliography.* Jefferson, NC: McFarland & Company.

Rudman, Masha Kabakow. (1984). *Children's literature: An issues approach.* Second Edition. New York: Longman.

Short, Kathy G. & Pierce, Kathryn M. (1990). *Talking about books.* Portsmouth, NH: Heinemann.

CHAPTER 3

Can I Really Make This Work? Strategies for Creating a Caring Environment

It is important to teach values to children as an integral part of the school curriculum as well as in their everyday home life. To make this happen, the entire classroom or home atmosphere must be one that is conducive for children to develop moral values. Both environments must be accepting and caring ones in which children feel they belong and are valuable members of the group.

The following chapters will provide you with teaching ideas for specific books. In this chapter, we share with you some ideas we have found successful at a more general level. The moral qualities adults can foster in children are many and various. Because this book is devoted to the use of literature, we have focused on those qualities best represented in available books. In the early stages of our writing, we considered a chapter on *friendship,* until we discovered that friendship was an underlying theme running throughout all the other issues. The values this book focuses on— *self-esteem; responsibility; sharing; truthfulness; solving conflicts peacefully; respecting and appreciating others; ecological values; diligence, perseverance, and patience; and unconditional love*—are of great importance in drawing friends into one's life.

Here, then, are ideas for creating the right parenting and teaching atmosphere. They are listed under each of the topics you will read about in coming chapters.

SELF-ESTEEM

Self-esteem is not a moral value, as such, but we have chosen to focus considerable attention on it because underlying all moral and ethical behavior are people's feelings about themselves. If people feel unworthy and undervalued, they sometimes seek power over others or become depressed. If they feel cheated, they may seek revenge. But if they feel confident, competent, and worthwhile, they seek positive actions toward others. They are more disposed towards moral growth.

To help children feel good about themselves, adults need to value and show interest in children's play and work. Two behaviors militate against the development of self-esteem: generic praise and criticism. Generic praise confuses children and makes them dependent upon others for their feelings of worth. Both parents and teachers often praise by saying, off-handedly, "Good boy" or "Good job." The child may completely misinterpret the message. The adult may mean, "I really like the way you picked up those toys and put them away," while the child thinks the adult is saying, "You're a good person and I like you a lot right now." This interpretation opens the door to feelings of insecurity. "If she likes me now, will she like me later? What do I have to do to get her to say that again?" Even though the toys have just been picked up and it is obvious and clear to the adult that there is a relationship between the comment and the behavior, the child may not get the connection. Making the compliment explicit helps the child understand more clearly as well as feel more secure.

Sometimes it is necessary to be critical of a child's behavior. Just as generic comments can cause confusion and insecurity in a praise situation, they may also do so during these more difficult interactions. It is important to be specific. Additionally, there is less confusion and insecurity when the child's entity is separated from the child's behavior.

For example, a parent might say, "In this house lights must always be turned off if no one is in the room." To be avoided is a personal attack such as, "You never will learn, will you? You want to pay the electric bills for me?"

A teacher comment might be, "The math books need to be put back on the top shelf and the manipulatives on the bottom. That way, the next children know exactly where to find things." Children are publicly humiliated by comments such as, "You kids in the Tiger Group put the books in the wrong place again. The five of you had better start paying better attention." While such public humiliation may temporarily assuage the teacher's anger, it does nothing in the long run to make children feel good about themselves. And children who lack such self-esteem tend not to improve their behavior.

A powerful way to promote self-esteem in children is for adults to encourage them to take risks. We communicate to children that taking risks implies the possibility of mistakes or even failure, and that neither is necessarily bad. Suzanne tried telling her third graders that risks were good and mistakes were all right, but most of them didn't believe her, possibly because their second grade teacher had emphasized perfection and a predictable curriculum. So, Suzanne started making "mistakes" herself and would follow them by such announcements as, "Well, I tried using the new paste but it's stickier than the old. I guess I didn't do a very good job. I'll have to try again." Sometimes she would add, "Even teachers make mistakes, don't they?"

Children began to feel more free about experimentation. The approach was so successful that once, when she really did accidentally drop an entire drawer full of school supplies, two children said loudly and in unison, "Teachers sure make mistakes, don't they?" Everyone laughed and Suzanne knew that risk taking had become a classroom ethic and that the children felt pretty good about themselves. She also felt a little better about dropping the drawer.

As children grow up they become aware of others and realize that they are unique. They need to feel positive about their unique qualities. Adults can do a lot to help children feel special. Never compare one child to another or hold one up as an example for the other to follow. Emphasize unique qualities and let children know that you love and appreciate those differences. Children are often in a rush to grow up. They need to be satisfied with their present condition and not always restless for the future. Encourage children to take risks. Let them know that even if they make mistakes you still love and appreciate them.

A large factor in one's self-esteem is having vision for one's life in the future. Individuals who have clear long-term goals in life tend to be more successful in all aspects of their lives, including moral development. It can be beneficial to help children project the effects of their actions upon their future lives and to think about setting long-terms goals.

The children's books we found on the topic of self-esteem clustered into four groups. In some books the story characters came to terms with their own uniqueness and felt better about themselves as a person even if they were different from others. Other books showed how story characters did not need to change in order to be successful or happy, but could be accepted and loved just the way they were. Several books said it is all right to have emotions—to be angry or afraid, and to hate to do things. Last, in quite a few books the smallest story character outwitted or cooperated with others to be a key factor in accomplishing something. Children reading these books could feel good about being physically small.

RESPONSIBILITY

Children can learn responsibility if adults force it on them in an authoritarian way. This method, however, is likely to produce rebellion when adult backs are turned and creates children with an external locus of control. Such children always rely upon others to make decisions and blame others for what happens in their lives. These children feel worthless and powerless and therefore cannot act responsibly. To teach responsibility so that constant supervision isn't necessary, children need to be given some measure of freedom and they must know that they are trusted. Cooperative activities, daily responsibilities, and empowering children with reasonable choices are important ways to encourage an internal locus of control.

Part of having an internal locus of control is to be able to solve one's own problems and children can begin to achieve this at an early age. Tattling to adults and expecting to be rescued by them develops an external locus of control by showing children they are incapable of making decisions that affect themselves. Instead adults should teach children to analyze their problems.

Freedom and trust underlie the parental philosophy of Joe Richards toward his son Jason. Last summer Jason announced that he'd like to earn more money than his home duties were paying him. He suggested mowing neighbors' lawns. Jason had just turned 11, and Joe was concerned about his safety if he were left alone with the family's large gas lawn mower. At the same time, he approved of Jason's initiative and wanted to support him. So, Joe found a hand mower at a garage sale and gave Jason his permission.

As a parent, Joe believes that a child's freedom has to be earned. Thus, he accompanied Jason on his first jobs, helping him mow at a professional level of competence. Soon, Jason was on his own and much in demand for his responsible approach to work. It is apparent, from his outgoing manner and self-confidence, that Jason knows he is trusted to do his best.

Children can be given more responsibility at school than is normally the case. In Japan, for example, children scrub down their entire school themselves before they go home each day. With this much student investment in the building, it shouldn't be surprising that vandalism is almost nonexistent. Care of the classroom can be promoted in any country at any age. Even very young children can be trusted to clean and polish safely.

When giving children responsibility, it is important to give them the amount for which they are ready. At home, preschoolers can help set the table for dinner; kindergartners can help clear; elementary children can be expected to help cook. At school, all ages can be expected to put materials away when they are finished, but elementary children can clean and put in order just about everything. Children who are given too much responsibility for their age feel burdened and afraid. Children who are given too little become self-centered and selfish. It is important, too, that children aren't given responsibilities for "make-work" jobs that are not really needed. They need to know they are making a real contribution.

The children's books we found on this topic give several reasons why story characters behave responsibly. Sometimes an emergency causes people to reach out and take responsibilities they might not otherwise assume. Story characters responsibly carry out household chores and family responsibilities. Children need to take responsibility for their own actions instead of blaming others. All of these themes occur in real life as well as in children's literature.

SHARING

If parents want to foster sharing at home, they must begin by setting the appropriate example. If children see parents acting selfishly toward neighbors, friends, and each other, the children's behavior is likely to be about the same. If home is a place where much is expected to be shared and all are expected to be responsible in the care of those things that are shared, family harmony can increase. Of course, there will be some things that are individually owned and it is important that everyone respect that also. Both children and adults can have places that are off-limits to others, and everyone, even the youngest, should understand that items in these places cannot be touched without permission.

Alena is a single mother with an eight-year-old son. Not long ago she observed that he was becoming increasingly selfish about his possessions. Friends lost their enthusiasm for coming over, but Max didn't seem to mind. He played alone quite happily, usually singing to himself as if to prove the point.

An enlarged family seemed to Alena the ideal solution to Max's behavior, and she decided to accept a foster child into the home. Although the going was rocky at first, the necessity of sharing when there were more people around helped Max grow out of himself. Alena also spent time explaining to both boys the ways in which she, too, shared. Although the foster child has now been adopted by another family, Alena still sees the progress Max made and his friends are beginning to return. Just to be sure, she continues to explain to Max when she shares something with him.

At school, children must also learn to share while still respecting others' property. If you are familiar with Montessori schools, you know that there are numerous, meticulously cared for learning materials. Careful observation of these materials, however, shows that there is usually just one of each item. The philosophy is that it is not as necessary to have sufficient materials so that everyone can do what they want when they want, as it is to provide an environment that forces children to learn to share. Much time is spent training the children to respect each other's interest in and use of the materials while also learning to share unselfishly.

Parents and teachers who model sharing and patiently promote it with their children usually notice that generosity is contagious. The resulting atmosphere is harmonious and happy. Children's books on this topic show how story characters decide to share toys or food. Reasons given for sharing include to meet a need, to distribute something, and for pleasure.

TRUTHFULNESS

Very young children cannot always separate fact from fantasy and sometimes their tall tales of what they have or have not done reflect this inability. By elementary school, children can be expected to understand the difference and to learn the adult meaning of truthfulness. Parents and teachers can foster this value by making truthfulness more attractive to children than lying. If children are continually afraid of adult anger or punitive consequences for their actions, they are more likely to lie as a means of self-preservation.

Lucy and Frances have been close friends for years and they each have two elementary-aged children who enjoy playing with each other. One summer day the four children played out in back of Frances' house while the mothers sat inside talking. Before long there was considerable commotion followed by the breathless arrival of four very wet and chagrined children. Each child raced to his or her own mother to report that their overenthusiastic use of the plastic swimming pool had put a large leak in it.

Lucy fairly screamed at her children, even calling them "stupid." As she did so, their story of the experience began to change, with Frances' children emerging as the villains. Meanwhile, Frances kept calm, held each of her children's hands, and asked for an explanation. Her children were visibly upset by the screaming coming from the other side of the room, but they told a quite different story of joint responsibility. Subsequent checking showed, of course, that their story was the more accurate one.

Frances is a teacher and she told us this story when we asked her how she fosters truth-telling in her first grade class. "Whenever I'm inclined to get angry about something going wrong, or impatient with children's fighting, I remember this experience. Scaring kids is no way to get the truth out of them. It's funny. Lucy's kids are actually more polite than mine. They are required to 'yes, Ma'am' her and they do it well. But I've heard them talk about her in really nasty ways behind her back. I know my own two don't do that. If they're unhappy, they tell me to my face." Frances grinned a bit. "Of course, I'd sure like it if my kids were more polite. I haven't figured out how to have it both ways though."

The children's books that we found on truthfulness had themes involving stealing, telling the truth, and being obedient. All depicted story characters who got into trouble when they were not honest or obedient. In addition, there are a number of trickster tales where good prevails over evil, but only by devious means. Children can benefit from analyzing these tales to think about the difference between tricking, joking, or teasing and being dishonest.

SOLVING CONFLICTS PEACEFULLY

Many conflicts at home and school arise because of misunderstandings concerning responsibility and sharing. If parents and teachers focus on these, perhaps using the ideas we have suggested, many conflicts will be resolved easily. Again, parents and teachers can foster harmony by setting appropriate examples themselves. This does not necessarily mean they must hide their conflicts from children. Inevitably the time will come when adult conflicts will be observed. That is the time when adults must work their hardest to come to peaceful conclusions. It will be helpful to share with children the way in which this was done. At home a parent might explain, "Mom and I both wanted the car, but we've decided to take turns. That way it's fair to both of us." At school, an example might be, "Mr. Templeton said we were singing too loudly, but he agreed with me that we need to enjoy our singing. So, we're going to sing while his class is outside at recess. Then we won't bother his class."

Shannon Jones, a second grade teacher, actively teaches proactive classroom management strategies to her class. The students brainstorm possible ways to solve a problem. Shannon invites students to fill out index cards with their names on one side and a problem that bothers them on the other. Each morning Shannon selects a card and that student selects a partner to act out a possible solution. The rest of the class offers other possible solutions. Role playing helps the development of children who know what to do but are not at the stage to respond appropriately without thought.

Joe Richards (you met him above) is on his second marriage and determined to get it right this time. He and his wife are in agreement that it's better for Jason to know that parents fight than to believe that adults can always get along. They don't purposefully argue in front of him, but if they sense that he has observed a disagreement, they explain to him the way in which they resolved it. This has had an unexpected benefit: Joe and his wife know they had better resolve an argument well if they expect to tell Jason about it!

In order to solve problems skillfully, children must see themselves as capable people who have significance. If they are permitted to decide the logical consequences for misbehaviors in the classroom or home this attitude will be encouraged. Resentment can be avoided if these standards are set by the class or the family before typical problems occur. Logical consequences must be related to the problem, respectfully dealt with, and reasonable to ensure that the solutions are logical consequences and not punishment. Literature contains logical consequences occurring to story characters which can provide excellent models and situations for discussion.

For example, in the children's book, *Rachel and Obadiah,* by Brinton Turkle (Dutton, 1978), the logical consequence of Obadiah's taunting of his sister and stopping to pick blackberries is that he will lose the race with her and not get to carry the message about a ship's arrival to the captain's wife. Children might discuss Obadiah's decisions to make fun of his sister and stop to pick blackberries instead of completing the race. What were the alternatives available to him at the time? What might have been a better course of action? Children can then relate this situation to one in which they have teased a sibling or a classmate and the consequences that ensued.

Children can be taught about natural consequences—standing in the rain and getting wet, touching a hot stove and getting burned, or not eating and getting hungry. Experiencing these consequences teaches us how to avoid unpleasant or painful situations. The same is true for logical behavioral consequences. Children understand that if they throw sand, they can't play in the sandbox; if they misbehave at lunchtime, they will have to eat lunch at a table by themselves. These consequences are meant to teach children to avoid inappropriate behaviors and take responsible actions, not to serve as a punishment. If children are punished with a consequence that is not related to the misbehavior (such as staying in from recess or missing a family outing because of hitting someone), their external locus of control will continue to develop as will resentment towards adult authority. A plan which can be written or drawn according to a child's developmental abilities is shown below:

Today I had a problem. I've decided to make a plan because I don't want this problem to continue. My problem is _____.
This problem would not have happened if I _____ _____. Next time I have this problem I will _____.
If I don't follow my plan a logical consequence will be _____.

Children's books on solving problems peacefully show how story characters have dealt with jealousy, including the arrival of a new baby, sibling rivalry, and friends quarrelling over toys. Arguments involve anger, name calling, and petty bickering. There are a number of books about bullies. These books provide clear and vivid examples for children of how problems can be solved peacefully.

RESPECTING AND APPRECIATING OTHERS

Respect is most readily taught by adult example. A parent or teacher can preach about brotherhood and loving others who are different, but their behavior is what children notice. Even the youngest child picks up the message from a snide comment or a cynical look. We all have prejudices, although we often don't permit ourselves an awareness of them. It is important for us to face our feelings squarely and then deal with them.

Alan Ackerman is principal of a private school where most of the children are high achievers who come from economically privileged families. Several years ago he determined that there would be benefits from increasing the diversity within the student population. He approached the faculty and the students about including children with disabilities in every class. The children were openly enthusiastic and entered into immediate discussions about what they could do to make the experience a good one. While the teachers also stated their enthusiasm, the principal sensed that all was not well. At a faculty meeting, his queries finally yielded some hesitancy on the part of a few teachers to having disabled children in their classrooms. As one said, "If I wanted that kind of trouble I'd have stayed in public school." From this revelation followed a series of discussions and some in-service from trained professionals. Not until all the teachers felt comfortable did Alan signal the county office that everything was ready for the children's arrival. After one year, every teacher proclaimed the experiment a success and it continues to this day.

Children must also be permitted to face their negative feelings about others rather than being forced to submerge them without discussion or explanation. "Don't call him that. It's not nice" is a directive that has no carryover to other situations. Leslie, a third grade teacher, has a brief time after lunch each day when children share their concerns and feelings about anything they like. She finds that this is sometimes a vehicle for expressing antagonistic attitudes toward, or puzzlement about, different groups. Leslie believes that, because the atmosphere of the class is so accepting, children sometimes make statements or ask questions that they might not at home. Every attitude is dealt with honestly and the children help each other overcome prejudices just as they do other problems.

Cindy Willis helps her kindergarten students develop empathy, respect, and appreciation for others by making laminated circles with different faces drawn on them. If a child feels especially happy, sad, angry, or has had hurt feelings, he or she may take a feeling face and sit in a designated chair. The class has been trained to ask the person, "What's wrong?" or "How can I help?" When a student sits in this chair others offer comfort or share in his or her joy.

Sharon tries to help her children learn to love and appreciate her neighbors. At Halloween her children invite some friends over to carve pumpkins for the senior citizens in their neighborhood who would otherwise not have Halloween decorations. Her daughter, who studies piano, occasionally visits a lady who was formerly a professional violinist so that they can play for and with each other. The family makes it a point to greet hikers and bikers as they pass the house. These friendly behaviors demonstrate to the children that it is rewarding to be friendly to everyone.

Many wonderful children's books involve story characters and settings that are multi-cultural. Exposure through books to individuals who have a culture different from their own helps children learn tolerance and even appreciation for different cultures and life styles. Several books directly confront the moral issues of prejudice. Many books show story characters being kind and caring toward people who are different from themselves, especially senior citizens and those who are disabled. Several books just celebrate diversity.

ECOLOGICAL VALUES

The coming generation has developed the most intense ecological awareness and ardent concern for the environment. Parents everywhere have received reminders from their children to do a better job of recycling everything or to conserve water and electricity. Of course, it is adults who have made them aware in the first place, but children have somehow made the issue their own. With a little effort, teachers and parents can support their interests and encourage the development of ecological values.

Glenda Parks' first grade class read *Miss Rumphius,* by Barbara Cooney (Viking, 1982) and discussed ways they could make the school grounds more beautiful. Committees were set up to plant flowers around their portable classroom, water the flowers regularly, and keep the weeds pulled. The children took pride in creating a more beautiful environment and learned that hard work coupled with responsibility learned in their jobs was a real key to the success of their garden. These values will probably be carried on for a lifetime by these children.

Boots Aryis' multi-age class of learning disabled students went beyond their classroom to set up a recycling program for their community. They received a state award for their ecological contribution to the environment. These children collected thousands of aluminum cans and newspapers, establishing habits of recycling for themselves and benefitting their community as well.

At home we can explain to children what we are doing and why we are doing it. "I am turning off the lights in this room because we want to save electricity" lets children understand why we behave the way we do. Often our actions are unnoticed or misunderstood, so, if we want children to learn from what we do, explanations are helpful.

Children can obtain needed information about the environment from nonfiction books. But they also need to develop attitudes which affect their behaviors toward the environment and these are frequently depicted in fiction books. Books with environmental themes inspire us by sharing the diversity of life supported by different habitats. Many feature extinct or nearly extinct animal species and call for preservation of that animal. Although most are rather one-sided in their presentations, several directly address environmental issues from more than one point of view.

DILIGENCE, PERSEVERANCE, AND PATIENCE

These traits have not been much in evidence in recent years in our society of job hopping and easy mobility. Yet, they are often crucial in getting a job done or accomplishing an important goal. It is important to communicate to children that perseverance is not always easy, but that it does have rewards. Comments such as "I'm sure glad to be finished with all that cleaning. It took a long time, but now I won't have to do any more of that kind of work for another whole week" can help children see that adults, too, would like to give up sometimes and that there can be satisfaction in not succumbing to the temptation to quit.

In his fourth grade class, David likes to balance the work between long-term and short-term projects. He feels that the latter make the former easier to sustain for the time that's necessary. Sometimes he permits the children to choose which work will take longer. For example, a lot of personal writing as well as factual reporting takes place in his class. Each week the children choose one or two pieces of work that they would like to expand upon and polish to perfection. These projects can take two weeks or more to complete, but the children rarely complain, probably because they choose the work themselves.

Perseverance to a very young child is quite a different concept. One mother we know tried hard to teach her two-year-old to pick up toys but all he did was cry. Finally, she started to do it with him and he began to help quite happily. For a child that age, even three minutes can seem like a very long time and picking up toys an overwhelming project. If parents and teachers carefully observe where children are in their development, they can encourage them appropriately to increase their capabilities in diligence, perseverance, and patience.

Parents and teachers can encourage children to complete projects and activities that they start. They can promote some long-term projects or reasons to save money over time to encourage patience. It has been shown that people with long-term goals are the most successful in life. Having vision, dreams, and an agenda for the future is an important reason to be diligent and to persevere.

Diligence in children's literature appears in daily activities, in tackling a challenging problem and sticking with it to a conclusion, and in being patient, or waiting, which is a very difficult thing for most children to do. Biographies show the tenacious behavior of those heroic individuals who have made noteworthy contributions to the world. There are books with story characters who try to do something that is very difficult for them or work very hard at a project. Several books show story characters exhibiting very patient behavior as they wait for something.

UNCONDITIONAL LOVE

We sometimes define this value as love that is given away without any concern about receiving a reward in exchange. Reaching this goal is a mark of maturity but children can, and must, begin progress toward it if their lives are to bring satisfaction. Perhaps this value, more than any other, is taught best by adult example.

Shirley Cochran, a reading teacher, shows her students unconditional love by listening to them. Each class session she lets her students express especially happy or sad things happening in their day. By listening to students and taking them seriously we allow these students to feel worthwhile and, coupled with the feeling of unconditional love, actions such as power struggles, attention seeking, or revenge do not occur.

Parents and teachers model unconditional love when they behave as was suggested in the section, "Self-Esteem." If an errant child's behavior is separated from the child, he or she is more likely to still feel loved. A parent, particularly, is in a position to state, "I still love you, but I don't like what you have just done."

In fact, parents should let children know quite regularly and very directly that they are loved. They need to actually hear themselves say those important words, "I love you," rather often. At the same time, they should not be said so often and with so little meaning that children feel insecure. When children feel loved themselves, they more easily learn to love others.

They are also more likely to be able to cope with the many difficulties life may send their way. Lisa considers herself extremely fortunate as a mother because her two teenagers have turned out to be extraordinarily normal. To see why this is cause for celebration, listen to the interview she did with her 17-year-old son.

It took place one evening over some shared ice cream on the back porch. It suddenly occurred to Lisa that some of her friends wouldn't even know where their sons were at that moment and she said, "Could I ask you something? How is it that you've turned out okay? Your parents have been separated twice and divorced once. You've been moved back and forth across the country several times, changing schools and leaving friends you care about. Your father has gone to prison in a case that was on television for everyone you knew to see. And yet, you don't use drugs, rarely drink, your grades are excellent, you're loving and loyal to your friends, and most of the time you're happy. Do you have any idea how those happened?

"Gosh, Mom," he laughed, "You make it sound like my life has been horrible!"

"Well," Lisa answered," a lot of kids would say just that if they'd had your experience. And they'd be in a psychiatrist's office trying to figure out how to deal with it.

After a few moments of thought he said, "I can think of just one thing. Both you and Dad have always let me know that you always supported me and loved me. No matter what." The old saying that "love conquers all" may be an exaggeration, but as Lisa's experience shows, it can go a long way toward helping children overcome much that is negative. It apparently helped Lisa's son learn to love despite many negative experiences.

If adults design their classrooms and homes to be caring communities where each child feels significance and belonging, then children will be on their way to acquiring the strategies necessary in our society to become successfully employed, have satisfying family and social lives, and be a part of a more caring community and a more peaceful world.

CHAPTER 4

Self-Esteem

RATIONALE

The coming chapters of this book focus on specific issues in children's moral development. Each chapter suggests ways in which children can be encouraged to demonstrate the positive qualities that pertain to it. Basic to all of these, however, is the need for children to have a good measure of self-esteem. Children behave more responsibly and at higher levels of moral development when they feel good about themselves. For example, a child who feels that no one loves her enough to give her the things she wants and needs will find it difficult to share happily. Children who are harshly punished and denigrated when they make mistakes will have little motive to be truthful. A child whose family is in constant conflict and physically abusive of him will have a hard time relating to the idea that conflicts should be decided peacefully. Children who are not respected and appreciated by others or given the unconditional love they need will have no understanding of what it takes to express these qualities to others. Children who are told repeatedly that they are failures will have no reason to believe that diligence and perseverance can lead to success.

Children need to feel good about being unique and special. They need to feel good about their looks, their behavior, and their friends. When children feel good about themselves, they are less likely to follow blindly what others say and do. High self-esteem has been linked to success in school. Children who believe they are good, competent people do well both academically and socially. We all need to be sure that we let children know they are fine and successful the way they are. We need to help them grow in a positive way, encouraging them warmly while, at the same time, not shrinking from giving them honest advice and direction.

Books in this area of moral development focus upon several themes. One is that it is all right to be different from your family or friends. By reading these books children see that being different is good, but the classroom extensions must help children relate to the storybook character in order for children to relate that character's experience to their own. Several books indicate that even when things don't go well or as you planned, you are still an OK person. Quite a few books face the issue of self-esteem head on and share how each person is special and unique. Often young children feel powerless in a world of bigger and older individuals. A theme in a number of stories is that being little is important after all.

CLASSROOM VIGNETTE

Children who accept their unique individuality and feel good about themselves have high self-esteem. *Frederick*, by Leo Lionni (Knopf, 1967) is an excellent book for sharing a child (or, in this case, a mouse) who is very satisfied with being different from his siblings. As the field mice gather supplies for the long winter, Frederick doesn't help. Instead he sits quietly gathering sun rays, colors, and words to brighten the winter days.

As Kathy read *Frederick* to a class she paused to ask, "How do you think the other mice feel about Frederick not working?" ·

"Sad," "Angry," "Like I want to tell him he's gotta work because we are" were some typical responses.

She asked the same question after Frederick cheered up the long winter days.

"Happy" and "not mad any more" were two responses.

Patience is a key concept in *Frederick*. Often times we jump to prejudiced conclusions and make degrading comments about others. This story helps us understand how good things sometimes happen from things we don't expect.

The class completed a writing experience telling how they could be more like Frederick in the classroom. The writing was illustrated and shared with the rest of the students. Each child told what he or she could do to help make the classroom a nice place to be. Typical responses included "help someone," "share," "be nice on the playground," and "cooperate with the group."

BOOK REVIEWS AND CURRICULAR EXTENSIONS

In the following bibliography, the grade-level designation "P" means the book might be most valuable for the primary grades, kindergarten to grade 3. The designation "I" means the intermediate grades 3-5.

Adoff, Arnold. (1991). *Hard to Be Six.* Illus. by Cheryl Hanna. Lothrop, Lee & Shepard. P, 32 pages.

A six-year-old boy reflects upon how difficult it is to be six on the day of his sister's tenth birthday. The frustrations of being six—not being able to run as fast or eat as much as the older children, pinning the tail on the donkey's foot, falling off a bike—are counterbalanced by the good feelings he gets when he plays in a muddy corner of the yard with his trucks, pretends to be a fire chief under the bed covers, plays with his mother, and gets new shoes.

Most children are in a hurry to grow up. It helps them to appreciate being the age they are by looking back at what they can do now that they couldn't do just a few years ago. Children can create "I can . . . . but I can't . . ." pictures and writings to reflect upon just where they are in the process of growing up.

Allinson, Beverley. (1990). *Elfie.* Scholastic. P, 32 pages.

Elfie is different from all the other ants in her community. She has a loud voice that makes others run away from her. The plasticine art illustrations make Elfie and her fellow ants seem alive. In the end, her strong voice saves the lives of the rest of her family and they come to accept her differences.

Children who are different can appreciate how Elfie feels when she is rejected by her family and friends because of her loud voice, which she cannot seem to control. Children can talk about how frustrating it is to be different and to have others not understand those differences. As a class they can discuss how to accept someone with a hearing loss, a vision deficiency, or other characteristics that make them different.

Browne, Anthony. (1985). *Willie the Champ.* Knopf. P, 32 pages.

In an earlier book, *Willie the Wimp* (Knopf, 1985), Anthony Browne introduces the character of Willie who is definitely the nonviolvent type. In this second book, focusing even more on self-esteem, Willie likes to read, listen to music, and walk in the park with his friend Millie. He is no good at "boy-type" activities like soccer or bike racing, and his friends tease him at the pool and when he cries at the movies. This sensitive young man encounters Buster Nose, the neighborhood bully, but instead of running away as the neighborhood children do, he stands against a wall. When Buster throws a mighty punch, Willie ducks and Buster slams his hand into the wall. When Willie stands up he slams his head into Buster's chin. Buster is in great pain. Willie apologizes and Buster goes home to his mom. The rest of his friends place Willie on their shoulders and call him, "Willie the Champ." A smiling Willie is obviously feeling good about himself.

This book not only glorifies nonviolence, but also shows how a sensitive child can feel good about himself even if he isn't talented in traditional activities typically enjoyed by his sex. Being different from other boys is just fine. Children can reflect on those things they do that are different from other children and how it makes them feel to succeed in ways that are different from common activities for their sex.

Bryan, Ashley. (1989.) *Turtle Knows Your Name.* Atheneum. P, I, 32 pages.

This tale from the West Indies is about a boy who has a very long name, Upsilimana Tumpalerado. He works persistently to learn how to say his name (which relates to Chapter 11 of this book on diligence, perseverance, and patience), and when he finally succeeds, he and his grandmother celebrate. But his friends still can't remember his name—except for turtle. Turtle makes Upsilimana Tumpalerado feel good about his long name.

Names are very important to children, and related to their self-esteem. Children can research the origins of their names and share their findings with others in their class.

Cameron, Ann. (1988). *Most Beautiful Place in the World*. Knopf. I, 64 pages.

Juan lives with his grandmother in San Pablo, Guatemala. His parents have abandoned him, so he works as a shoe-shine boy in order to earn his keep. Yet Juan dreams of going to school one day. Eventually he learns to read and realizes that where he lives is, indeed, the most beautiful place in the world.

Children need to feel good about themselves and where they live even if they live in a less than favorable environment. This book might help children look at the beauty around them and identify what is good about their lives.

Carle, Eric. (1984). *The Mixed-Up Chameleon*. Harper. P, 32 pages.

The chameleon doesn't know who he is or what color he should be. He sees parts of all different animals that are attractive. Eventually he adapts his colors to his surroundings, making himself a bit like each of the other animals whom he admires.

A story of identity, this book can help children reflect upon who they are. Are they like their mother? their father? other people? Yes, but they are unique as well. Children can fold a drawing paper in half. On one side they draw themselves as unique (perhaps using many colors) and on the other side as like everyone else (perhaps in just one color). They can write about how they are like each member of their family and then how they are unique.

Cohen, Barbara. (1991). *213 Valentines*. Illus. by Wil Clay. Holt. P, I, 55 pages.

Wade, an African-American boy, has to transfer from his beloved Roosevelt to Kennedy School to participate in the gifted and talented program. He's not sure he belongs and is convinced that he will not receive any valentines except from the one person who drew his name; so he purchases 200 valentines and sends them to himself and a friend, under the names of famous people. A chapter book that is easy to read, this book would be ideal for children in second or third grade.

Children can recall those feelings of concern at Valentine's Day when the popular children receive lots of cards and those who are less popular receive fewer. They can talk about how it feels to be popular or less popular and what makes children "fit in." Role-playing the opening of Valentine's Day cards might trigger discussions and strategies for helping all people in the classroom feel wanted, needed, and appreciated.

Croll, Carolyn. (1991). *The Three Brothers*. Putnam. P, 32 pages.

In this German folktale, the youngest brother longs to play an important role on the farm like his older brothers. Their father designs a contest to see which son will inherit his farm. It will be the son who can fill the barn to its fullest in the course of a day. The oldest son quickly herds the animals into the barn. The middle son fills the rafters with hay. By the time the youngest son gets a turn it is already evening. Yet his candle lights the entire barn completely and quickly, so he wins the contest.

Younger children will eagerly tell or write about the times they have tricked their older siblings. They might list all the ways they are made to feel small, young, and even inferior to their older siblings, and then share their lists with the children in the class who are older siblings with younger sisters and brothers.

Ets, Marie Hall. (1978). *Just Me.* Penguin. P, 32 pages.

A very simple repetitive text tells how a child pretends to be each of the animals in the barnyard. She flaps her wings like the goose, lies near the mud like the pig, and so forth. In the end, she is just herself, and is obviously happy that way.

Children might think about and discuss how they are like other people, and then how they are unique. Class charts and graphs might depict some of the similarities: children who play soccer; children who play musical instruments; children who take karate. There could also be a chart on "How We Are Unique," which the children sign and then list their unique traits.

Freeman, Don. (1964). *Dandelion.* Viking. P, 32 pages.

Dandelion is invited to Jennifer's party and decides to get all spruced up for the occasion. He has his mane curled and buys new clothes, but when he arrives at the party, Jennifer doesn't recognize him and closes the door in his face. A rainstorm returns his mane to its natural state, and when Dandelion returns to the party he is welcomed with open arms. Dandelion states the moral of the story: "From now on I'll always be just plain me!"

Children need to feel satisfied with who they are and how they look. The children might generate charts which they sign when they agree that "It's OK to be tall; It's OK to be short; It's OK to be large; It's OK to be small" and other aspects of their appearance.

Glen, Maggie. (1990). *Ruby.* Putnam. P, 32 pages.

Ruby's paw is stamped with an "S" at the toy factory. She thinks "S" stands for "special," but the other "S" teddy bears tell her she is a "second." "We're mistakes," explains a teddy with rabbit ears. Ruby is not content to be thrown out, so she masterminds an escape. Ruby finds her way to the best toy shop in town, where the other toys make fun of her. A girl named Susie is shopping with her grandfather and selects Ruby precisely because she is different and special. "It has character," explains the child when the shopkeeper offers to substitute a perfect bear for the "second."

A comparable book is *Corduroy* (Viking, 1968) by Don Freeman. Corduroy is bought by a girl even though he is missing a button on his overalls. Younger children can talk about what makes their teddies or stuffed animals special. Older children can discuss the implications of labeling things or groups of people. Children with obvious disabilities might share how it feels to be "special" or different.

Graham, Amanda. (1987). *Who Wants Arthur?* Gareth Stevens. P, 32 pages.

Arthur, a dog, sits day after day in a pet shop window watching people selecting other pets. When Arthur sees that fish are popular, he tries to act like a fish. He pretends to be all sorts of other animals, but it is not until he becomes himself again that he is selected as a pet.

This book can help children learn to be satisfied with who they are. The class can draw names, and each person then makes a list of positive attributes about the name he or she has picked. The children might also write about why they like to be themselves.

Greenwald, Sheila. (1980). *It All Began with Jane Eyre*. Little, Brown. I, 128 pages.

Franny Dillman's mother tries to convince Franny to read more "normal" novels because the classics she reads by flashlight in the closet set her imagination to working overtime. Franny, however, realizes that she has little in common with the characters in contemporary realistic fiction books. This hilarious account of a child who enjoys reading classical literature and then applies what she is reading to her own life reaffirms for older children that it is all right to be different. Franny stands up for her beliefs and does not cave in to her mother's pressure to be like other teenagers.

Upper elementary or middle school students might discuss those qualities that all human beings share, regardless of when they lived or who they were. Perhaps some of them, like Franny, can identify with story characters from previous centuries more easily than with their contemporaries. Sharing these feelings in school can help older children deal with the changing aspects of their lives.

Hooks, William H. (1989). *The Three Little Pigs and the Fox*. Illus. by S. D. Schindler. Macmillan. P, I, 32 pages.

The female runt of the litter is the one who outwits the fox and saves her bigger brothers in this Appalachian version of The Three Little Pigs. This story will be enjoyed by young children who are often in the runt's position. A chart which shows all the powerful and intelligent things they can do despite their size can contribute to their self-esteem.

Isadora, Rachel. (1976). *Max*. Macmillan. P, 32 pages.

Max is a great baseball player; his sister, Lisa, takes ballet. On Saturdays Max walks Lisa to her ballet lesson on the way to baseball practice. One Saturday Max has extra time and his sister invites him to participate in ballet class. He is hesitant, but joins the class and finds that he enjoys it and can perform rather well. He decides that ballet is a great way to warm up for his baseball games.

Boys in the United States are rarely encouraged to be graceful and there tends to be a stigma attached to boys who enjoy participating in activities traditionally enjoyed more by girls. This book can help children analyze their own feelings about boys doing girl-type things and vice versa. Children could each make a list of the types of things that they enjoy which would normally be enjoyed more by the opposite sex. The teacher can invite a ballet teacher into the classroom to teach all the children how to dance—or the physical education teacher can include ballet as a part of the physical education curriculum.

Klass, Sheila Solomon. (1991). *Kool Ada*. Scholastic. I, 176 pages.

Being a new child in school is hard enough, but when one moves from a rural, southern, mountain home to the north, problems of adjustment are compounded. A compassionate, yet firm teacher is the one who helps Ada figure out that her rough exterior and temper are not permanent solutions to her adjustment problems.

Children might see the resemblance between Ada and Gilly in *The Great Gilly Hopkins,* by Katherine Paterson (Crowell Jr., 1978). Both are strong-willed, wise, misfit individuals who overcome their social problems in the course of a touching story. Children can talk about how it feels to be a misfit and how to befriend those who are different. One class made a list of all the ways each class member was unique from the others, which helped everyone feel good about being different. Those with talents shared them with their classmates.

Lane, Megan Halsey. (1990). *Something to Crow About.* Dial. P, 32 pages.

Cassie, a chicken, and Randall, a rooster, each wanted to do what the other could do. Cassie could lay eggs and Randall could cock-a-doodle-do. In the end they realized that "being different was *really* something to crow about."

This is a very easy predictable book with lots of picture clues that kindergarten children could read independently and to each other. They might list things they could do well and write a "Something to Crow About" book about themselves. (Be sure they really understand what this expression means. Give them an opportunity to role-play proud crowing.) If portfolio assessment is being used in a classroom, the showcase portfolios are places where children can put papers that are "something to crow about." In a more formal lesson format, children could list things they do well, then team up with another person who can do things they can't and follow the book's model for writing their own versions. A group chart of things each child can do well will let children see what they are best at.

Leaf, Munro. (1936). *The Story of Ferdinand.* Illus. by Robert Lawson. Viking. P, 48 pages.

Ferdinand the bull likes to sit and smell flowers instead of butting and bullying the other little bulls. When the man from the bull ring comes to select a bull for fighting, all the others try to impress him, but Ferdinand sits next to some flowers. The only trouble is that he sits on a bee, and the jumping and wild behavior that ensue convince the judges that he belongs in a bull ring. He does not. In the bull ring all he does is smell the flowers in the ladies' hats.

Children can discuss what they like to do that is different from everyone else. They might talk about a time when they were "out of character" for an unusual reason, as happened to Ferdinand. This can be followed by encouraging children to create illustrations of themselves in these experiences. Older children might make paper dolls and dress them in and out of character.

Levine, Ellen. (1989). *I Hate English.* Illus. by Steve Bjorkman. Scholastic. P, I, 32 pages.

A child who is being tutored in English because English is her second language has a very poor attitude about learning the language because she sees no need to learn it and because English is such a hard language to learn. After working with her very patient tutor she begins to feel better about speaking her native tongue and about acquiring a second language.

Children know that sometimes learning something new is hard, perhaps becoming an experience they hate. This book helps them understand that accomplishing something difficult can make them feel good. Many children whose second language is English feel inferior to children who are native speakers of English. A classroom that encourages talk in children's first languages, and helps everyone in the class learn other languages, helps build the self-esteem of children whose second language is English. If there are bilingual children in your classroom, have them teach something of their language to the rest of the class.

Levinson, Marilyn. (1991). *The Fourth-Grade Four*. Illus. by Leslie Bowman. Henry Holt. P, I, 64 pages.

Alex Burman is enjoying fourth grade. He is on the soccer team and has some good friends. The announcement that he needs glasses threatens his peace and happiness, for he thinks he may no longer be able to play soccer and that his friends will make fun of him.

Lots of children have faced getting glasses, braces, or other physical adjustments and can write and talk about how those experiences made them feel. The class can discuss the roots of relationships and the difference between physical appearance and behavior as a cause for friendship. They can also talk about and perhaps role play how it feels when people get teased about something.

Lionni, Leo. (1969). *Alexander and the Wind-Up Mouse*. Random House. P, 32 pages.

Alexander meets Willie, a wind-up mouse, and becomes dissatisfied with his life, preferring to be loved by a human as Willie is. Alexander takes steps to transform himself into a mechanical mouse, only to find that Willie has been discarded and is no longer loved by his owner. Being a live mouse doesn't seem so bad after all.

This story is a clear example of the grass being greener on the other side of the fence. Children can discuss times when they have wanted or still might want to be like someone else. They can list the satisfying aspects of their lives. Younger children could make simple charts: I am happy about . . . I am sad about . . . .

Milhouse, Katherine & Dalgiesh, Alice. (1990). *The Turnip, An Old Russian Tale*. Putnam. P, 32 pages.

In a cumulative tale, each person who helps pull the huge turnip out of the ground is unsuccessful until the very end. When a mouse helps out, the turnip finally comes out of the ground.

This book can be used with young children in conjunction with William Hooks' *The Three Little Pigs and the Fox,* to demonstrate the power of the smallest member of a group. Children might list the advantages of being small—things you can do because you are small that larger people can't do.

Peet, Bill. (1986). *Pamela Camel*. Houghton Mifflin. P, 48 pages.

Pamela Camel thinks poorly of herself because she is considered the stupidest animal in the circus. It is not until she runs away and saves a train from destruction that she begins to feel good about being a camel. To honor her heroism the circus owners place her first in the circus parade.

Children can think of one thing they do well that makes them feel good about themselves. They can write about it and draw a picture. Younger children may enjoy replicating the circus parade, marching with their pictures held high. Older children might select one thing they don't like about themselves and then explore ways they might alter that character trait.

Polacco, Patricia. (1990). *Just Plain Fancy*. Bantam. P, 32 pages.

Naomi isn't satisfied with the plain ways of her Amish family. She complains that everything is so plain and tells her little sister that just once she would like to have something fancy. While she collects eggs from the chickens, she notices one that is spotted, different, and more fancy than the rest. She places it under a hen, and when it hatches it produces an unusual looking bird. In the meantime, Naomi has learned about the Amish tradition of shunning people who are too fancy, so she worries that her fancy bird will be shunned. Instead, the bird, which turns out to be a peacock, is viewed by the elders as one of God's miracles.

This story about a child who is dissatisfied with who she is will ring true to many children. It is their family traditions that make children feel like valued members of the community. In fact, Naomi is so good with the chickens that she is eventually honored for her hard work. A class might take time to honor each child in the room for something special that child has accomplished.

Rodgers, Frank. (1988). *Who's Afraid of the Ghost Train?* Harcourt Brace Jovanovich. P, 32 pages.

Robert gets teased by his friends because he is afraid of everything. His vivid imagination just runs away with him. His Grandpa Jim, a former lion tamer, gives him a good idea for handling his fears. He tells Robert that he just pretended those large lions were big babies. At the carnival the next day, Robert tries this technique when riding the Ghost Train. He imagines what the ghosts would look like first thing in the morning. Much to his surprise, his friends are scared of the ride, but he wouldn't mind taking it again.

Children can talk about things that scare them and how they handle their fears. It is all right to be afraid sometimes. It happens to everyone.

Seuss, Dr. (1990). *Oh, The Places You'll Go!* Random House. P, I, 48 pages.

This best-selling book predicts nothing but success for the reader. A great esteem builder, the rhyming text explains there will be problems along the way, but in the end, life will be the way you want it to be. A very positive thinking sort of book.

Children could discuss times when they have been at the "waiting place" mentioned in the book, or when they have soared high, or had their balloons popped. Life does have its ups and downs, but for the most part it can be a happy experience. Children can share their dreams for the future and write short, encouraging verses for each other. These can be collected in a class book.

Thomas, Patricia. (1971/1990). *"Stand Back," Said the Elephant, "I'm Going to Sneeze!"* Illus. by Wallace Trip. Lothrop. P, 48 pages.

In a rollickingly funny rhyming narrative, the animals implore the elephant not to sneeze, because the last time he did all kinds of crazy things happened. The bears lost their hair, the bees lost their stingers, the birds lost their feathers, and so forth. It is a mouse who surprises the elephant and keeps him from sneezing, thus saving all of the animals from their embarrassing responses to his sneeze. However, the elephant ends up laughing, which is almost as bad as sneezing for the animals.

The powerful little mouse influencing a large elephant contains the moral that being small does not mean being powerless. Children can make a list of all the small things that they know about that accomplish powerful things, such as car door openers. They can relate these powerful situations to times when they were needed to help carry something heavy, prop up a collapsed bed, or open doors for someone.

VanLaan, Nancy. (1990). *A Mouse in My House.* Illus. by Marjorie Priceman. Knopf. P, 32 pages.

In rhyming verse, a child tells about the many different animals in his house, but really, each animal is himself! For example, one stanza reads: "A pig is in my house, and it's pink like a posy. There's a pig in my house, and it acts like me. It chomps and it burps as it begs for two desserts. There's a pig in my house, only I can see." In the last stanza a zoo is in the house, all wrapped up in one boy. This child feels so good about himself that he can laugh about himself even if he is greedy, sloppy, messy, and so forth.

A good book link would be Audrey and Don Wood's *Quick as a Cricket* where animal traits are again given to a child. Children can list their best attributes and those they would like to change. Using the book's format each child can write a similar verse about himself or herself. These can be assembled into a class book.

Viorst, Judith. (1972). *Alexander and the Terrible, Horrible, No Good, Very Bad Day.* Illus. by Ray Cruz. Atheneum. P, I, 32 pages.

Everything goes wrong for Alexander from waking to find gum in his hair to his cat not wanting to sleep with him at night. He decides that he is going to move to Australia to escape his problems. His mom assures him that some days are like that, but it is nothing to worry about.

Who hasn't had a terrible, horrible, no good, very bad day? Children can share some of the worst days in their lives. It helps to know that other people have bad times too, but that problems do get solved. Children can brainstorm what to do when they are having a bad day. Is escaping the answer? What are the alternatives? How can a very bad day be turned into a very good one?

Waber, Bernard. (1972). *Ira Sleeps Over.* Houghton Mifflin. P, 48 pages.

Ira is invited to stay over night next door at his best friend Reggie's house. He can't decide whether to take his teddy bear, Tah Tah. He is afraid that Reggie will make fun of him for sleeping with his teddy bear. When the lights go out, and they are all settled in to sleep, Reggie quietly pulls his own teddy bear out of a drawer of his dresser and admits to Ira that his teddy's name is Foo Foo. Much relieved, Ira runs home to rescue Tah Tah and bring her to Reggie's for the night.

Many children have teddy bears or other cuddly animals that provide them with comfort when they are going to sleep. Other children suck their thumbs for comfort. Children are sometimes embarrassed when these behaviors last into the elementary grades and beyond. Yet children need to know that it is all right to develop a deep attachment to one's thumb or a stuffed animal. There is nothing wrong with needing comfort when you fall asleep. Interesting small group discussions can emerge from sharing strategies for getting comfort just before sleep.

Wildsmith, Brian. (1979). *The Lion and the Rat.* Oxford. P, 32 pages.

A tough lion, the King of Beasts, finds himself caught in a net trap. A tiny mouse is able to extricate the lion with its sharp teeth and save his life.

Mice are known in literature for their powerful behavior in scaring elephants and in gnawing rope traps to save lions or other animals bigger than they are. The mouse-hero is a good example of small beings who are powerful, intelligent, helpful, and needed. Compare this story with Robin Ravilious' *Two in a Pocket*

(Little, 1991), where a mouse frees a wren from a net trap. Children can talk about when they have felt trapped and someone smaller or younger has helped them out. Or they can recall the gallant behaviors they engaged in when they were younger and smaller.

Winthrop, Elizabeth. (1980). *Sloppy Kisses.* Illus. by Anne Burgess. Macmillan. P, 32 pages.

Emmy Lou decides that she no longer wants to experience her family's sloppy kisses because her friend Rosemary says that sloppy kisses are for babies. For several days, Emmy Lou will only accept pats on the head instead of sloppy kisses. Her family doesn't understand, but they support her decision and go right on expressing their normal affections to one another. One night Emmy Lou can't sleep. Nothing helps her but a sloppy kiss. It is then that she realizes that being from a family that kisses a lot is not something to be ashamed of. As she enters school the next morning she proudly lets her Dad give her a sloppy kiss right in front of Rosemary.

Children might think about how their family is unique. What does their family do that other families don't do, and does that give them positive feelings or negative ones? Class discussions might include ways families prepare and eat meals, travel to and from work and school, and spend time together. Children can see that all families are different and better appreciate the specialness of their own families.

Wood, Audrey & Wood, Don. (1982). *Quick as a Cricket.* Child's Play. P, 32 pages.

A child notices how he is as quick as a cricket and as slow as a snail. Throughout the book there are opposites that describe the child's character. In the end, as with Nancy VanLaan's *A Mouse in My House,* all the traits together make the child.

Children can relate to the changes in the child, who is at one time quick and at another, slow. All children change character from time to time and place to place. There could be some wonderful discussions of times when they felt happy or sad, big or little, fast or slow. A class book might be compiled with the title, "We Are Quick as a Cricket," where children write and illustrate times they have behaved in these different ways.

Yashima, Taro. (1955). *Crow Boy.* Viking. P, I, 32 pages.

For six years, Chibi walks to school from the distant countryside. The children in his class make fun of him because of his rural dress and shyness. Finally, his kind sixth grade teacher encourages him to perform in the school talent show, and Chibi's unique qualities are at last appreciated. Because he can simulate the many different calls of the crows, whom he hears on the walk to school, the children affectionately name him, "Crow Boy," and their attitudes toward him change.

Children can write about people whom they know and who are different, especially if they have grown fond of someone who is different from themselves. They can identify their own hidden talents and share them. They can invite into the classroom individuals in the community who have unusual hobbies or life experiences.

Yorinks, Arthur. (1988). *Bravo Minski.* Illus. by Richard Egielski. Farrar Straus Giroux. P, 32 pages.

Minski is a scientific genius. His father parades him around Europe showing off his remarkable talents. But when Minski hears an opera star he is determined to invent a solution which will give him a beautiful voice. His father objects to his musical intentions seeing them as impractical and unworthy compared with his scientific genius, but Minski charts his own course and becomes a talented and famous musical performer.

It takes strong self-esteem, especially for individuals who are artistic, to reject roles that are commonly considered to be masculine, feminine, or practical for the less financially rewarding careers in music. Yet children must feel successful and worthy no matter where their talents lie. Children can write about why they like doing their special activities and share these good feelings with others in their classes.

Zolotow, Charlotte. (1972). *William's Doll.* Illus. by William Pene du Bois. Harper. P, I, 32 pages.

William desperately wants a doll. He has a basketball and a train set that his father has given him. His brother thinks he is a creep, and the boy next door calls him a sissy. Only his grandmother understands how he feels and so she brings him a baby doll to hug so that he can practice for the time in his life when he will be a daddy.

Boys need avenues to express nurturing tenderness, and dolls are one way to encourage that behavior. Teachers can encourage boys to play in the dressup area by announcing that there need to be some dads over there, and by providing anatomically correct multi-racial dolls. (Boys might prefer playing with boy doll babies.) One teacher had a man come in and diaper his tiny baby. The teacher bought some very small diapers for the children to use in the housekeeping area with their dolls. Boys might bring to school and share their special dolls and stuffed animals.

SUMMARY

Books that would be appropriate to share with children to enhance self-esteem fall into several categories: children accepting their own unique characteristics, books about identity, and stories in which the smallest character accomplishes an important task. Several help a child feel good about being different from others. *Frederick* gathers sunshine and colors instead of food for the winter; Franny reads classics instead of the more popular realistic novels in *It All Began with Jane Eyre*; Ferdinand smells flowers instead of fighting in *The Story of Ferdinand*; Alex needs glasses in *The Fourth-Grade Four*; William wants a doll to play with instead of more typically boy-type toys in *William's Doll*; Max finds that he enjoys ballet in *Max*; Willie enjoys reading and listening to music and is terrible at soccer and bike racing in *Willie the Champ*. Naomi wants something fancy instead of being plain like her Amish family in *Just Plain Fancy*; *Ruby* is made of leopard fir; Chibi and Ada come from the country instead of the city in *Crow Boy* and *Kool Ada*; and Emmy Lou learns to enjoy sloppy kisses instead of pats on the head in *Sloppy Kisses*. With the exception of Frederick and Ferdinand, most of these books are realistic stories about real people.

Children need to realize that they can be angry (*Alexander and the Terrible, Horrible, No Good, Very Bad Day*), be afraid (*Who's Afraid of the Ghost Train?*), hate to do things (*I Hate English*), and be different (*213 Valentines*) and still be competent, capable, well-liked individuals. Stories written in the first person speak directly to children about their own experiences and feelings.

In several stories children are led to see that their identities are unique. There are ways they are like other people and ways they are special. In *The Mixed-Up Chameleon*, *A Mouse in My House*, *Quick as a Cricket*, and *Just Like Me*, children are compared with others and in the end realize that they are different from anyone else. The child in *Turtle Knows Your Name* is different because of his very long name. An ant's voice is too loud in *Elfie*.

The message behind *Something to Crow About* is that it is important to feel good about being yourself. The child in *Most Beautiful Place in the World* dreams of going to school, but comes to realize the beauty in his own home. Arthur, in *Who Wants Arthur?*, Pamela, in *Pamela Camel*, and Alexander, in *Alexander and the Wind-Up Mouse*, think that they have to change in order to be accepted or happy. They learn that just being themselves gets them plenty of notice from other people. Minski chooses a musical career over a scientific one in spite of the objections of his father in *Bravo Minski*. *Dandelion* realizes that it is fine to be himself and he does not need to change or become fancy to please his friends. The ultimate esteem building book is *Oh, The Places You'll Go!* by Dr. Seuss.

Another group of books on self-esteem focuses upon small people or animals who achieve great things. The message is that size isn't everything. In *The Three Little Pigs and the Fox*, *The Turnip*, *"Stand Back," Said the Elephant*, and *The Lion and the Rat*, it is the smallest animal who is the most important. In *The Three Brothers*, it is the youngest son who wins the father's challenge. *Hard to Be Six* presents a more balanced view by telling how being six is difficult in comparison with what older children can do, but is better than when the child was younger. *Ira Sleeps Over* shares how hard it is to outgrow habits that are perceived by others to be babyish. Sometimes young children feel powerless in a society where everyone is older and bigger than they are. Teachers who are sensitive to their need for power arrange their classrooms to allow children many choices and to give children many responsibilities for daily tasks. Parents provide similar experiences at home, permitting children to make many of their own decisions and offer real help (not invented "make work") in the care of the house.

CHAPTER 5

Responsibility

RATIONALE

Part of being moral and ethical people is being responsible for our actions. It is especially important, in a democracy such as ours, to think and act rationally about the consequences of our behavior and to be accountable for our actions. However, thinking rationally, considering consequences, and accepting accountability requires a mature level of thought. These capabilities do not always come naturally to children and, without training, children can quite easily grow into irresponsible adults.

Before children are six or seven their thinking is nonrational (not irrational, which is quite a different thing), but in elementary school they begin to develop logical thought. This opens the way for consideration of consequences, previously a difficult thought process. It is important for teachers and parents to capitalize on this stage in development because, if they don't, their children may linger in this childish stage forever. The prisons are full of people who thought and behaved irrationally because they didn't take the time to think of the consequences of their behavior. Unfortunately, these same people are often unwilling to be accountable for what they did. Thus, they can never know the strength and independence that come from maturely taking responsibility for their thoughts and actions.

It can be a difficult task for adults to foster responsibility. Children are often quick to blame others for their actions. ("He started it!" "I only did that because she did it first!") They respond to a class assignment by saying, "This is stupid" or "I don't want to do this," when actually they mean, "If I try, I might fail and have to accept the responsibility myself, something I'm afraid to do because it would destroy my self-esteem." Blaming others is seen as a way to avoid punishment, but it also leads to an abdication of both responsibility and power over one's own life. If everything is in the hands of others, children need take no responsibility for their own actions. They become dependent in a society that requires independence.

Children who believe in hard work and their own effort as a determinant of their success work on an internal locus of control. They feel empowered and responsible for their own behavior. These children will take risks, try new things, and, when they don't work out, will mop up the spilt milk. They admit when they have made a mistake or done something wrong, and take steps to correct their errors. They feel confident in their own abilities to take care of themselves and be helpful to others.

Children need to learn that responsible people not only think through decisions rationally, consider the consequences of their behavior, and accept accountability for their actions, but they care for one another too. They respect the rights of others. In a classroom, this is translated as considerate behavior. Children talk softly so they don't disturb others who are working. They don't bump into people because that would be an inconsiderate action. They make supportive, cooperative statements instead of critical and taunting ones. The whole classroom involves having children think and behave responsibly and assume ownership for the classroom and its atmosphere. At home, considerate behavior includes respecting the privacy of siblings and not touching their possessions without permission, helping out with household chores without being asked, and obeying the rules of the family. When children are held responsible for the decisions that they make, they learn to see themselves as responsible, capable people who have some control over the events in their lives.

Examples exist in literature of story characters acting responsibly and receiving the natural and logical consequences of their actions. Story characters in the books reviewed below act responsibly while doing daily chores, while caring for younger siblings, and when facing emergency situations. Additionally, several books present the consequences of acting irresponsibly.

CLASSROOM VIGNETTE

It is easy to procrastinate. Waiting for the last minute to do a job usually results in doing an overwhelming amount of work in a short period of time. How can we help children understand that working on homework or chores a little bit each day is a lot less painful than an all day studying or cleaning session? Kathy explored this question with a class of second grade students.

In *Clean Your Room, Harvey Moon!* by Pat Cummings (Bradbury, 1991), Harvey wants to watch the morning cartoon shows but his mom says he can't watch television until after he cleans his room. In this fascinating rhyming story, Harvey Moon spends the entire morning tackling his messy room. As he finally finishes his room he hopes to catch the two o'clock "Caveman Capers" cartoon, but his mother has different ideas. After lunch she tells Harvey he has to clean the lumps, hidden toys, and shoes from under the covers on his bed.

This book is excellent to use in helping children gain an appreciation for taking responsibility to pick up their rooms every day and also for achieving high level responses to literature. Children tend to give more thoughtful responses when they can relate a story to their personal lives, and Harvey Moon is certainly a book which relates to children's lives. One of the most important things in a child's life is his or her bedroom. "Can you tell us about your room?" Kathy asked. The second grade students were very honest and sometimes a little embarrassed when telling others about the uncleanliness of their rooms. The students drew pictures of their rooms and wrote down ways they could avoid being like Harvey Moon. This information was shared in small groups, with other children offering added suggestions.

Responsibility must be taught and encouraged on a daily basis if we expect children to learn to take the initiative. Otherwise, we may find that, as they grow older, we must harangue, bribe, or plead to get them started on projects. Since most child-centered classrooms tend to be messier than most teacher-centered classrooms, Harvey Moon also provides an example for keeping the classroom tidy and orderly. It is easier to find supplies and move about safely in an unlittered room with orderly storage. Children can have "Harvey Moon time" once a day, probably at the end of the day, to be sure they are leaving the room the way they want it to be the next day when they come back to school.

BOOK REVIEWS AND CURRICULAR EXTENSIONS

In the following bibliography, the grade-level designation "P" means the book might be valuable for the primary grades, kindergarten to grade 3. The designation "I" means the intermediate grades 3-5.

Aardema, Verna. (1975). *Why Mosquitos Buzz in People's Ears.* Illus. by Leo and Diane Dillon. Dial. P, I, 32 pages.

This tale explains why mosquitos buzz in people's ears. The cumulative plot involves a mosquito talking to an iguana, who plugs his ears and then scares a python into hiding in a rabbit's den, which scares the rabbit, which causes a crow to cry out, which frightens a monkey, who bumps a dead tree limb, which falls and kills a baby owl. Each of the story characters denies responsibility for killing the owlet, and accuses another animal of the crime.

Although this is a silly fictional tale, the animals stating that it was not their fault is the same as a common phrase heard in classrooms and homes. Children can talk about finding solutions to problems rather than attaching blame for them. They can enjoy other cumulative tales where one character's action precipitates a domino effect.

Ackerman, Karen. (1990). *Just Like Max.* Illus. by George Schmidt. Knopf. P, 32 pages.

When Uncle Max, an immigrant tailor who lives and works upstairs in a tenement, has a stroke, his nephew looks after him in a most responsible way. He helps move his uncle from his upstairs room down to a lower floor so that his family can more easily care for him. He sits by his uncle's bed and spends time with him. Eventually he brings the man's sewing machine down to his bedroom, and, under his uncle's supervision, makes a dress for his mother.

When relatives become ill children often have to accept more responsibility. Children can relate examples of how they have pitched in when the need arose. They can brainstorm ways they might help out in the case of an emergency. If there is a nursing home close by, children might even assume the responsibility of visiting a patient on a regular basis or volunteering to help out at meal time.

Arnold, Tedd. (1988). *Ollie Forgot.* Dial. P, 32 pages.

Ollie has a difficult time remembering anything because little rhymes keep wandering through his head and divert his attention from the three grocery items his mother requested when she sent him to the market. Ollie's adventures are humorous and his determination to remember and complete his task is strong. In the end he behaves very responsibly and brings home the joint of beef, wedge of cheese, and loaf of bread that his mother had requested.

Children might discuss strategies they use to remember things, since remembering is part of behaving responsibly. They can also recall experiences they have had when being sent to the store to shop on their own.

Baker, Barbara. (1991). *Oh, Emma.* Illus. by Catharine Stock. Dutton. P, I, 96 pages.

Nine-year old Emma lives in a crowded housing development and longs for a home and a room of her very own. Her dreams are dashed when her parents announce that another baby is on the way. Emma learns to put her family's needs ahead of her own dreams and acts in a most responsible way as she overcomes her disappointment.

Many children have experienced the new responsibilities that come with the arrival of a new baby. They can discuss this and other family situations which draw upon them to be more responsible than they have been in the past. They might also discuss the satisfaction that comes from being responsible.

Birdseye, Tom. (1988). *Air Mail to the Moon.* Illus. by Stephen Gammell. Holiday. P, I, 32 pages.

Ora Mae Cotton blames everyone else in her family for stealing her tooth after it falls out and disappears before she can place it under her pillow. She seeks out her Mama, her Dadaw, her brother, and her sister, vowing to send the rascal that stole her tooth "air mail to the moon." At the end, she has to bear the responsibility for the missing tooth herself; it has been in the pocket of her pants the whole time.

Ora Mae mentions how embarrassed she feels (like a zebra without stripes; like a possum up a plum tree) when she discovers her error. Children might enjoy recounting their embarrassing moments, or the times when they have accused others, only to discover that the error was their own.

Brett, Jan. (1991). *Berlioz the Bear.* Putnam. P, 32 pages.

Berlioz the Bear has a buzzing sound coming from his double bass, but his orchestra is late for its performance so he doesn't have time to investigate what is causing the problem. En route, he steers the mule driving the wagon with the orchestra on it into a ditch. All of the players try hard to solve this problem and pull the wagon from the pit, but their efforts are to no avail. The humorous twist at the end has a bee extricate itself from Berlioz's bass and sting the mule, causing him to pull the wagon to the plaza for their concert.

Children can relate this story to times when they were late or had to solve difficult problems responsibly. The idea of pulling together and cooperating is another issue worthy of discussion. Children might recall experiences when they helped others or someone helped them solve a problem.

Cazzola, Gus. (1991). *The Bells of Santa Lucia.* Illus. Pierr Morgan. Philomel. P, 32 pages.

Lucinda absolutely adores bells of all kinds that she hears in her village of Santa Lucia—cow bells, sheep bells, school bells, and the big grandmother bell in the village square. But Lucinda's grief at the death of her beloved Nonna makes it no longer possible for her to love bells anymore. It is not until the schoolhouse is on fire and she is forced to ring the bells in the village square that Lucinda has the courage to act responsibly, alert the village to the disaster, and thus overcome her own sorrow.

Emergencies require children to act in mature and responsible ways. Children can share how they have been responsible in past emergencies, and review the procedures for what they would do if an emergency, such as a fire, were to occur.

Chorao, Kay. (1988). *Cathedral Mouse.* Dutton. P, I, 32 pages.

A mouse who has been hunting for a safe haven, finds refuge in a cathedral, where a man visits him daily and feeds him bits of bread and cheese. Gradually, the mouse warms up to this caring man, who takes him to his workshop where he chisels stone statues. This kind man carves a statue of a mouse with a tunnel in it just the size of the mouse so that at last he has a home in the cathedral.

This touching example of a person providing food and shelter for an animal can be a springboard for discussion of caring for animals and the kinds of food and shelter animals require. It takes a lot of responsibility to care for animals, and children will benefit from hearing how their peers meet these responsibilities.

Dale, Penny. (1991). *The Elephant Tree.* Putnam. P, 32 pages.

In this fantasy picture book, Elephant wants to climb a tree. All of his friends (a teddy bear, a rabbit, a mouse, and two children) help him search for a tree in the backyard. They find everything but an elephant tree, and then decide to make one for the elephant, a very responsible way to help a friend in need.

Friendship is very important to children. They will enjoy sharing with others the ways they have acted responsibly in helping a friend in need. Class discussions can focus on how they might help other children who have needs. A "Dear Abby" box provides a vehicle for children to write anonymously about their problems and for the class to consider responsible solutions to them.

dePaola, Tomie. (1981). *Now One Foot, Now the Other*. Putnam. P, I, 48 pages.

After his grandfather suffers a stroke, Bobby helps him learn how to walk again.

Children can talk about ways they might help older people who have challenges to face. Perhaps the class could adopt a senior citizen who lives nearby and provide attention and care for that individual. Grandparents and great-grandparents would appreciate children writing to them, sending pictures, and generally caring for them, and all of these activities might take place in school.

Duffey, Betsy. (1991). *A Boy in the Doghouse*. Simon & Schuster. I, 96 pages.

George works hard at training his new puppy, Lucky, because if he doesn't get the dog under control, his parents have threatened to make him return Lucky to the pound.

Pets are a great responsibility. In a classroom you might have the children decide upon a class pet, earn the money to support it, and sign up for caring for it. At home, children who have pets usually share in their training and upbringing. Those with dogs might share how they have trained their dogs to be calm and respond when called.

Fox, Mem. (1985). *Wilfred Gordon McDonald Partridge*. Kane/Miller. P, I, 32 pages.

Wilfred visits the nursing home next door on a regular basis and enjoys all of its residents. His favorite friend, however, is Miss Nancy, who is losing her memory. In a touching story, Wilfred helps Miss Nancy recapture her memory of some wonderful life experiences she has had.

A class might adopt a nearby nursing home and make regular visits to the residents. Foster grandparent programs benefit both the grandparent and the children. Children can talk and write about their experiences with older people. They might invite older people into their classroom and learn to be considerate of their special needs.

Galdone, Paul. (1982). *Hansel and Gretel*. McGraw-Hill. P, 32 pages.

In this version of *Hansel and Gretel*, Hansel collects stones to mark the trail home from the forest for himself and his sister. Gretel responsibly gives Hansel some of her bread when, on the second time out, he uses his own bread as a marker for the path. Gretel cooks food for her brother who has been captured by the witch, and is the heroine when she pushes the witch into the oven and oblivion, and thus frees her brother. This book also demonstrates cooperation and sibling harmony.

Children who have siblings might tell or write about times when they have behaved responsibly toward their siblings and vice versa. You can discuss ways in which the classroom is like a family and list methods that your "Hansels" and "Gretels" can use to care for each other. Older children especially can relate to the concept of the entire world being a family. Taking on the responsibility of caring for less fortunate "brothers and sisters" may lead to participation in charitable organizations.

Galdone, Paul. (1968). *Henny Penny.* Seabury. P, 32 pages.

Henny Penny does all sorts of work cutting wheat, milling wheat, and baking the wheat into bread, and none of her friends volunteers to help her. In the end she eats what she has made right in front of them because they did not help.

Responsible farm animals or children do their part on projects. When assigning group projects, ask the children to write out their contribution. These descriptive writings about the project can be posted next to the project in museum fashion so that visitors to the classroom can understand what each person did to make the project a successful display. Children can have discussions about what to do with a person who does not do his or her part to contribute to group work, or the child who does everything all by himself or herself. Discovering how those behaviors make others feel can help the offending children reform.

It should be noted that a child who does all the work is depriving others of the opportunity to contribute, and some children may seek attention in this way. For older children, it is amusing and instructive to retell this story from the other animals' point of view. A useful contrast book is Barbara Baker's *Oh, Emma* (Dutton, 1991), where a child is responsible for chores and derives a sense of satisfaction from successfully completing her routine. These books emphasize the fact that responsible children (or animals) perform their chores in a cheerful manner.

Haas, Irene. (1975). *The Maggie B.* Macmillan. P, I, 32 pages.

Margaret Barnstable has a dream one night in which she is the captain of her very own ship, the Maggie B., and her darling brother, James, keeps her company. She responsibly cares for her brother by fishing, then cooking for him, bathing him, and singing him to sleep. She secures the ship during a storm and makes sure James is not afraid. The two enjoy a most delightful trip on the Maggie B.

Children often care for their younger siblings and pay special attention to them in an emergency situation like a storm. They can tell about their experiences and share ideas for how to help a younger sibling in emergencies.

Hazen, Barbara Shook. (1974). *The Gorilla Did It.* Illus. by Ray Cruz. Atheneum. P, 32 pages.

In this humorous fantasy story, a gorilla befriends a child who is trying to fall asleep and tempts her to play in a chaotic and destructive way. When her mom asks, "Who made this mess?" the child responds that the gorilla did it. The mother asks the child to think about what happened and then to come out and explain what really occurred. The child explains to the mother that the gorilla said he was sorry and helped clean up the mess.

Children can learn from this book to accept responsibility for their own messes and not to blame someone else. Lively discussions could result from asking children when someone has blamed them for something they did not do. Apologizing and cleaning up after making a mess are both responsible behaviors. This book might be referred to later when apologies for inappropriate behaviors are in order.

Hughes, Shirley. (1988). *Dogger.* Lothrop, Lee & Shepard. P, 32 pages.

After David loses his stuffed animal, Dogger, his sister Bella lends him one of her teddy bears. Shortly thereafter, when David spies Dogger for sale at a used toy stand at a carnival, he realizes that he doesn't have enough money to buy it back. When he can't find his parents, his sister responsibly helps him retrieve his prized stuffed animal from a little girl who has just bought him.

Children can recall times when older siblings or babysitters have "gone to bat" for them so that justice could be done. In addition to discussions of fairness that this book prompts, children can gain more empathy for David's predicament by talking about their prized possessions and what they would do if one were lost. Many children who have favorite stuffed animals have experienced their loss and can then better appreciate Bella's responsible actions.

Hughes, Shirley. (1984). *An Evening at Alfie's.* The Bodley Head. P, I, 32 pages.

When Alfie's mom and dad go out one evening leaving the children with Maureen, their favorite babysitter, the water pipes burst. Maureen and Alfie both act very responsibly. Maureen calls home and finally her dad comes over and shows her how to turn off the waterpipe at its source. She cleans up the mess as best she can. Alfie, who has noticed that his baby sister has been crying, comforts her and alerts Maureen to her need for a change of diapers.

Older elementary school children and middle school children probably have many babysitting tales to tell and write. They can discuss what they would do if a pipe burst while they were babysitting. You can invent other disasters and help children choose appropriate ways to deal with them or role-play what would happen if they occurred. Younger children can talk about how they responsibly help babysitters, especially in the care of younger siblings.

Hurwitz, Johanna. (1991). *School's Out.* Illus. by Sheila Hamanaka. Morrow. P, I, 128 pages.

Lucas Cott can't wait until school is out and he can take a real vacation from responsibility. But when his mother hires a French au pair named Genevieve to help take care of Lucas and his twin brothers, he thinks it will be like living with a teacher all summer, and plots mischievous things to say and do to take advantage of "General Genevieve." When one of his tricks goes too far, Lucas learns the importance of acting responsibly all the time, not just when school is in session and someone is watching over you.

Children will relate to two issues in this book. Many children are cared for by others while their parents work. These children can recall times when they have sabotaged babysitting efforts and times when they have acted responsibly while their parents were gone. All children can relate to school being out for the summer. The class could graph their plans for summer vacation and discuss any responsibilities they might have during the summer.

Hutchins, Pat. (1991). *Tidy Titch.* Greenwillow. P, 32 pages.

Titch's older brother and sister clean their rooms and give to Titch all of the toys they have outgrown, so that his room becomes all cluttered.

Like Harvey Moon in Pat Cummings' *Clean Your Room, Harvey Moon!,* these children are being responsible by cleaning their rooms. Children might talk about what they do with their toys when they have outgrown them. A class might even collect and repair old and worn out toys for needy children in the community.

Jeram, Anita. (1991). *It Was Jake!* Little, Brown. P, 32 pages.

When Danny is bored one day, he engages his dog, Jake, in some rather messy play. When his mother accuses him of making a mess, he blames it on Jake. They dress up, leaving clothes all over the floor; they dig holes in the backyard; and they wash up together. But when Danny blames Jake for cutting up papers, his mom points out that Jake can't use scissors, turn on faucets, hold a spade, nor dress himself. Danny's punishment is not logical. He is sent to bed without supper, but his mother relents and brings him a sandwich and some milk. Only it is Jake who eats the sandwich!

Children sometimes blame one another for things that go wrong. Sometimes their blaming behavior is as truthful as they can make it, but they often make assumptions instead of determining the truth before uttering accusations at one another. After reading this book, children can adopt Jake when they need to blame someone. This makes a situation less threatening. It is important to follow up the humorous situation by asking the child to tell what really happened. With possible anger dispelled, a child is better able to face responsibility. An accusatory classroom or home is not a very pleasant place to be. Children can learn not to tattle, but to find alternative strategies for clarifying situations. They must also be responsible for their own actions. There are strong similarities between this story and Barbara Shook Hagen's *The Gorilla Did It*.

Laird, Elizabeth. (1991). *The Day Patch Stood Guard*. Tambourine/Morrow. P, 32 pages.

Patch, a sheepdog, rides with his farmer, Stan, on the tractor to the top of a hill. When the farmer forgets to set the brakes on the tractor, Patch alerts him to the danger.

Children will enjoy studying animals who have responsibility for people, especially working dogs, such as guide dogs and sheep dogs. Children can relate any examples of responsible behavior their pets have demonstrated and gather articles from newspapers about responsible pet behavior.

Mahy, Margaret. (1991). *Keeping House*. Margaret K. McElderry Books. P, I, 32 pages.

Lizzie Firkin is a creative person who is too busy singing songs, writing, tap dancing, and playing the trombone to clean house. Her house is a royal mess. Only after she desperately calls Robin Pickertucker, the Wonder Housekeeper, does she discover that she can clean house very well when she wants to.

Children whose parents employ a housecleaning service can relate to all the housecleaning that gets done in preparation for the house cleaners to come. Others will relate to spring cleaning, or cleaning up for guests. In any case, children can share their home responsibilities and the feelings they derive from contributing to the welfare of others.

Mazer, Anne. (1991). *The Salamander Room*. Illus. by Steve Johnson. Knopf. P, I, 24 pages.

Brian finds an orange salamander in the woods and wants to give it a home. His mother's gentle, prodding questions have him creating such an elaborate habitat for the salamander that it becomes obvious to everyone that the salamander is more suited to his woodland home than to Brian's house.

This tender story about caring for wildlife might result in discussions about trying to tame wild animals and about the responsibility that accompanies caring for a pet. There are lovely ecological messages about the food chain and animal habitats as well.

McCloskey, Robert. (1952). *One Morning in Maine*. Viking. P, 32 pages.

Sal takes good care of her younger sister, Jane, on a shopping trip from the island where they live to the Mainland. When she and Jane are offered ice cream by a storekeeper, Sal tells him that Jane should get vanilla so that any drips won't stain. This experience and others demonstrate Sal's tender care of a younger sister and provide a lovely model of responsible behavior.

Children will have many sibling care stories to share. If the class has a buddy reading program with younger children, you can discuss the ways older children can do thoughtful things for the younger ones and be responsible for them when they are together. Field trips with two classes of different age levels provide wonderful opportunities for older buddies to care for younger children.

McMullan, Kate. (1991). *The Great Eggspectations of Lila Fenwick*. Illus. by Diane de Groat. Michael di Capua/Farrar Straus Giroux. I, 148 pages.

The school librarian attempts to teach sixth graders about responsibility by having each student care for a hard-boiled egg as if it were a newborn baby. Lila, who as usual is full of great ideas, finds that many backfire en route to learning a lot about being responsible.

Adopting an egg or a similar item might be an appropriate way for upper elementary children to replicate the experiences of the children in this book. Since many upper elementary children are beginning to babysit, a mini-unit on caring for young children would be appropriate.

Mendez, Phil. (1989). *Black Snowman*. Scholastic P, I, 32 pages.

Jacob learns to believe in himself and his heritage as he uses the magic of the kente, a cloth with wonderful powers, and a black snowman, to save his younger brother from a fire. A self-esteem theme pervades this book as well as the responsibility theme.

Children can talk about how their heritage helps them be more responsible and about acting responsibly during emergencies. All children have family heritage stories of bravery which can be retold to give children a sense of pride in who they are and in the actions of their family members.

Patz, Nancy. (1972). *Pumpernickel Tickle and Mean Green Cheese*. Franklin Watts. P, 32 pages.

This hilarious story shows how Benjamin takes Elephant, his imaginary friend, with him to the store so that he will remember what his mother asked him to buy. They make up rhymes and are silly and tease each other on the way to the store, and when they arrive, they have forgotten what it was they were to purchase. They have a minor disagreement, blaming each other for forgetting and calling each other names (fitting in with Chapter 8 of this book on solving conflicts peacefully), but finally remember the grocery list. Benjamin's mother is pleased when he returns with just what she has asked him to get.

Children enjoy doing errands for their parents and can talk and write about the errands they perform. Linking this book and Ted Arnold's *Ollie Forgot,* children can share ideas for remembering things.

Pryor, Bonnie. (1991). *Greenbrook Farm.* Illus. by Mark Graham. Simon & Schuster. P, 32 pages.

In this picture book, beautiful paintings contribute to the special caring attitude that a little girl has for the baby animals on her farm. She responsibly goes about her morning chores—tending the spring lambs, feeding a filly and Elsie's baby calf, and sprinkling corn for chicks and a family of ducklings. At lunch time she, her dad, and her older sister return home across the fields on a tractor to greet their tiny baby brother who is just awakening from a nap.

Of course no child would ever have all of these responsibilities for baby animals; yet the tender feelings in this book are ones which children can relate to. They can talk about how young animals and children need additional care and attention and ways they have or could provide that care.

Roos, Stephen. (1991). *Love Me, Love My Werewolf.* Illus. by Jacqueline Rogers. Delacorte/Doubleday. I, 128 pages.

The third graders form a Pet Lovers' Club and plan a Halloween party to raise money for the animal shelter. Bernie, one of the members, finds the courage to stand up to a class bully when he is teased for wanting a dog as a pet so much.

A trip to an animal shelter might be a practical response to this book. In doing so, children might learn a lot about responsible pet care. Children might like to band together to earn money for a worthwhile cause. They might also enjoy writing about how they care for their pets.

Sendak, Maurice. (1962). *Pierre.* Harper. P, 32 pages.

Pierre says, "I don't care," many times a day to each of his parents' suggestions. Finally, in this fanciful "cautionary tale," the parents leave and he ends up being swallowed by a lion. As he is retrieved from the lion's belly, he is heard to exclaim that he cares. To not care is irresponsible (and sometimes a defensive technique). To care is responsible.

Children are sometimes heard to exclaim, "I don't care." This book can help them realize the negative impact those words have on others. People like to be around others who are considerate and caring. A classroom might brainstorm all the considerate and caring things they can do in school. For example, how can they be more responsible and considerate in the media center, in the music room, or the art room? How can they be more considerate at PE? The "special" teachers will appreciate a more considerate class of children. How can we show that we are responsible for our own classroom? Do we handle materials carefully and keep the place looking tidy?

Van Allsburg, Chris. (1988). *Two Bad Ants.* Houghton Mifflin. P, I, 32 pages.

The scout ants announce that they have found a huge mound of delicious crystals (sugar in a sugar bowl) and the ant community sets out to retrieve them for the queen. Two bad ants decide to remain in the crystal pile instead of returning with the other ants. This is a terribly irresponsible action because the crystal pile is a most dangerous place for them to be. They suffer severe consequences for their actions, and in the end learn that being home and obedient is far more satisfying than taking unnecessary risks.

Children can recount tales of when they have done something dangerous. They can chart the possible consequences of some dangerous activities that they know to be wrong. Discussions can include drug education at older grade levels.

Wittman, Sally. (1978). *A Special Trade*. Illus. by Karen Gundersheimer. Harper. P, I, 32 pages.

When Nelly is little, Old Bartholomew, her neighbor, cares for her constantly— playing with her, pushing her stroller, helping her learn to walk, and encouraging her as she learns to skate. He is very responsible in his care for her, alerting her to when there are bumps in the pavement and helping her only when she needs it so as to encourage her independence. His model of responsible behavior is mirrored in Nelly's own actions when Old Bartholomew falls down and must be in a wheelchair. She carefully pushes him around, alerting him to the bumps in the pavement, and she holds his hand as he learns to walk, but only when he needs that assistance.

This is a lovely tale of intergenerational love and caring. Old Bartholomew and Nelly are not related. They are just neighbors and very good friends. Both are very responsible in their actions toward one another. School children can adopt a senior citizen or visit a nursing home on a regular basis to develop such relationships of their own.

SUMMARY

Children's books on the topic of responsibility tend to cluster into several groups. One way children evidence responsibility is by helping with chores. When they care enough to clean their room (*Clean Your Room, Harvey Moon, Keeping House,* and *Tidy Titch*), feed farm animals (*Oh, Emma* and *Greenbrook Farm*), shop for groceries (*Ollie Forgot* and *Pumpernickel Tickle and Mean Green Cheese*), help prepare food (*Henny Penny*), and respond to their parents (*Pierre*), they are responsibly fulfilling their role in a family or classroom. In *The Great Eggspectations of Lila Fenwick* upper elementary children learn about the responsible care of a baby. Negative examples, such as *Henny Penny, Two Bad Ants,* and *Pierre* can be as effective in discussing this moral issue as positive examples because they point out the consequences of being unwilling to accept chore responsibilities.

Children sometimes have difficulty admitting guilt. They try to cover up what they have done or to accuse others of doing what they have done in order to avoid punishment. *Why Mosquitos Buzz in People's Ears, The Gorilla Did It,* and *It Was Jake* all place the blame for their actions on others (animals, an imaginary gorilla, and a pet dog). Children need to learn to accept responsibility for their own actions. Ora Mae Cotton in *Air Mail to the Moon* accuses everyone in her family of stealing her lost tooth, and is embarrassed when she has to admit that it was in her pocket the whole while.

In our segregated society many children rarely have contact with older people. There are many books which demonstrate the responsible behavior of children toward the elderly and help break down ageism. In *Wilfred Gordon McDonald Partridge*, Wilfred helps a nursing home resident who is losing her memory remember some special times in her life. Bobby helps his grandfather learn to walk after a stroke in *Now One Foot, Now the Other*.

Emergencies often force individuals to act responsibly when they might not have otherwise. A fire triggers responsible behavior in *The Bells of Santa Lucia* and *Black Snowman*. A mule refusing to pull a wagon stuck in a rut causes the orchestra animals to cooperate in *Berlioz the Bear*. A stroke that incapacitates his uncle, causes a boy to act responsibly in *Just Like Max* and a fall causes similar behaviors for Nelly in *A Special Trade*. A witch's threatening actions in *Hansel and Gretel* spur Gretel to care for her brother. Other examples of responsible sibling behavior are found in *One Morning in Maine, The Maggie B,* and *Dogger*. A babysitter cares for Alfie and Annie Rose in *An Evening at Alfie's* and an au pair for Lucas in *School's Out*.

Caring for pets and wildlife provides many lessons in responsibility for children. In *Cathedral Mouse* a man provides food and shelter for a mouse. A boy thinks through what would be needed to care for a salamander in *The Salamander Room*. George trains his puppy in *A Boy in the Doghouse*. The children in *Love Me, Love My Werewolf* raise money for an animal shelter.

Friendships provide opportunities for children to practice responsible and caring behavior, as in *The Elephant Tree*. Lastly, a work dog provides an excellent example of responsible behavior in *The Day Patch Stood Guard*. One way to extend these books is to involve children in volunteer work caring for someone who needs help.

CHAPTER 6

Sharing

RATIONALE

Sharing is a major part of children's friendships. In Chapter 1 you read of William Damon's research on sharing which showed that children progress in stages as their understanding of this important value becomes more mature. Studies done by researchers who have followed Damon's model have shown that children's understanding and demonstration of sharing can be enhanced and fostered by teachers in classrooms.

Suzanne and Linda spent several weeks in primary classrooms using children's literature as a way to encourage sharing attitudes and behaviors. Children's moral reasoning is expanded through giving and hearing a variety of viewpoints at different levels of development. In the area of sharing it is interesting to hear the children discuss if story characters should or should not share and the reasons for their opinions. Moral growth can occur in these sessions, especially if the teacher acts as a facilitator and refrains from giving his or her opinion.

Some of the books and techniques Suzanne and Linda used are recommended in this chapter. One method was to read aloud to the children, conduct a guided discussion, and use drawing as a vehicle to focus their ideas. The younger children had difficulty concentrating on a discussion when their bodies needed something to do. So, drawing as they talked about the books centered the children's attention. Further, the illustrations would sometimes reflect the changing thought processes of the discussion itself. This occasionally meant that a picture began as a representation of one level of reasoning and, by the time it was finished, was demonstrative of more mature thinking. If you teach younger children you might consider this approach.

Suzanne and Linda also observed that the sharing theme of the stories was often reflected in classroom life, even during the discussions themselves. For example, one boy brought a large and beautiful box of markers to school and wanted to use them for illustrating during the discussion. Of course, the other children wanted to share, but he felt much more comfortable keeping them all for himself. The discussion at that moment departed from the story at hand and focused on the more real needs of the children. After the children convinced the boy that "it's good to share," he reluctantly agreed to do so. Previous to this day, he had been one of the most moralistic children during the discussions. Now, he had to learn the difficulty of real-life application. Whenever possible, give your children an opportunity to both discuss the literature and to put the ideas into practice. The two go hand in hand.

The ability to share is important both at home and at school. At home, if children have to wait for a turn at anything, it is usually for a brief time, but in school sharing takes on a whole different dimension. Taking turns and being patient, learning to negotiate with others so that things run smoothly and fairly, become important social learning experiences. Children need to learn how to become less egocentric, and to listen to others.

CLASSROOM VIGNETTE

Jeanette Hiebsch, a Chapter 1 teacher, read Laura Numeroff's book, *If You Give a Mouse a Cookie* (Harper, 1985) to her class and found it wildly popular. So, as a follow-up, she shared several other books on the cookie theme, and the class decided to hold a school-wide cookie baking contest. Judges, including the principal, custodian, and guidance counselor, rated the cookies and the winning class earned a cookie party. The cookies came from the contest and drinks were supplied by a local business, which also provided balloons and gift certificates. The beautiful part of this activity was that the Chapter 1 children really enjoyed the cookie books, found others at the library, and read them aloud in each class that participated in the contest. Thus, these developing readers had real reasons to read stories fluently. Further, there was a lot of literacy involved in the making of the posters, announcing the winners, etc. Since many of the children in this class were poor, it was an unusual opportunity for them to share with others. The host class got no party, no cookies, and no rewards other than the good feeling that came from putting on a party for another class. The class's nickname is Hiebsch's Heroes. One boy sighed after the party was over, "Mrs. Hiebsch, we really were heroes today!"

BOOK REVIEWS AND CURRICULAR EXTENSIONS

In the following bibliography, the grade-level designation "P" means the book might be more valuable for the primary grades, kindergarten to grade 3. The designation "I" means the intermediate grades 3-5.

Alexander, Martha. (1976). *I Sure Am Glad to See You, Blackboard Bear*. Dial. P, 32 pages.

Gloria has many excuses for not sharing her many toys until she discovers that if she will share she can play with another girl's magical bear. While adults may be uncomfortable with a moral based on self-interest, Gloria's reasoning is entirely appropriate for younger children. This is a good story for children in the lower grades to act out. They may even enjoy doing it several (or many) times.

Bishop, Claire Hutchet. (1952/1980). *Twenty and Ten*. Illus. by William Pene Du Bois. Viking/Puffin. I, 76 pages.

During the German occupation of France in World War II, 20 French children are living in a sanctuary in the mountains when they are asked to hide 10 Jewish children. Not only do they hide the children and protect them from the Nazis, but also they share their meager supply of food with them, involving difficult self-sacrifice on the part of all of the children.

This book opens the door to a discussion of how any class of children could share their wealth with the less fortunate children elsewhere in the world or even in their own neighborhood.

Brown, Marcia. (1947/1986). *Stone Soup*. Macmillan. P, I, 32 pages.

Some hungry soldiers pass a town and ask for a bit of food. They must trick a greedy townswoman into making soup for them by offering to provide her with stone soup. They plop the stone into the water, then declare that it would taste a bit better with a vegetable and some seasonings. Bit by bit the townspeople share what is needed to make the soup nourishing and palatable, all the while believing it is "stone" soup.

Children could discuss how much better everyone would have felt if the woman would have shared in the first place. They might also discuss what made the woman and the town so greedy. Were they afraid of hunger themselves? Younger children don't understand the trick in this story or the moral involved, so for them actually making the soup helps. Older children, however, find both the trick and the moral fascinating for in-depth consideration. Some children in one class made a sharing book. They drew pictures of what they liked to share and what they did not like to share and told why.

Carle, Eric. (1977). *The Grouchy Ladybug*. Harper. P, I, 32 pages.

The grouchy ladybug lands on a leaf with a friendly ladybug who offers to share some aphids. The grouchy ladybug refuses and asks the friendly ladybug if she would like to fight. She declines and he retreats, saying she is too small to fight anyway. The grouchy ladybug proceeds from animal to animal, asking each if it wants to fight. As the animals get bigger and bigger the situation becomes more absurd. Finally the whale flips the grouchy ladybug back to its original leaf, where the friendly ladybug has saved some aphids to share with the grouchy ladybug.

Children might create their own versions of "Grouchy Student" books in which they place personal experiences where friends initially have not shared, but later learned to share. Children might make lists of things that they own that they are willing to share and those they are not willing to share.

dePaola, Tomie. (1978). *Clown of God.* Harcourt Brace Jovanovich. P, I, 32 pages.

A poor boy finds happiness and success at being a travelling entertainer. He becomes a clown and juggles all sorts of different things. As he becomes older he starts dropping things and people laugh at him, so he takes off his costume and returns to the town of his birth. There in a cathedral is an unsmiling statue of Mary and her baby. The old juggler takes out his costume and puts it on for one last time to entertain the statue of the Holy Mother. This happy moment captures the end of his life, and he falls to the floor, dead.

Here is a man who gives his humor to the world all his life. Children will want to discuss how he felt when people laughed at him. They understand feelings of humiliation. They can relate that to children teasing and laughing at other children who are different. In the end though, this book demonstrates vividly how satisfaction comes from giving to others. A nice book link would be *Crow Boy*, by Taro Yashima (see Chapter 4 on self-esteem for a description).

Ferguson, Alane. (1990). *Cricket and the Crackerbox Kid.* Bradbury. I, 179 pages.

Two children both befriend the same dog in this book for upper elementary children. Even though the children have very different backgrounds, the dog links them and they end up sharing the pet.

Sometimes unusual circumstances force us to share something we love a lot. Children can discuss things they have to share, but would rather not. They can work on strategies to make such sharing experiences more harmonious.

Hogrogian, Nonny. (1971). *One Fine Day.* Collier. P, 32 pages.

In this Caldecott Award winning book, an old woman chops off Fox's tail because he spills her milk. When he asks for his tail back, she tells him that he must first return her milk. Fox proceeds from one individual to another requesting needed supplies in order to get the milk back. Each person or animal shares only in order to get something he or she wants. One child, after hearing this story, said he knew why the individuals didn't quickly share. It was because the fox didn't say "please."

This is another lower level, "you scratch my back and I'll scratch yours" example of moral reasoning which is very appropriate to use with younger children. The class might discuss why she would not sew his tail back on without the return of her milk.

Howard, Elizabeth Fitzgerald. (1991). *Aunt Flossie's Hats (and Crab Cakes Later).* Illus. by James Ransome. Clarion. P, 32 pages.

Aunt Flossie shares all of her old hats with her granddaughters who come to visit her every Sunday afternoon. Not only do the children get to wear these hats, they parade around in them and listen to Aunt Flossie's stories of the past and the places and times she wore those hats.

So many grandparents have a "do not touch" policy for anything in their homes and especially for their antique or personal possessions, but not Aunt Flossie. Never once does she say "be careful, now." That sharing attitude on the part of an older person who is a member of the family is very refreshing. Children can talk about things that trigger memories for old people they know. Telling stories is sharing a part of yourself from the past and giving children their rich cultural and family heritage. A follow-up activity would be for children to solicit stories from the older members of their families or friends and to ask to see the artifacts associated with those stories.

Hughes, Shirley. (1988). *Dogger*. Lothrop, Lee & Shepard. P, 32 pages.

When David loses his stuffed dog, his big sister shares one of her teddy bears until he can find Dogger. Her cooperative, sharing attitude makes David very happy and secure.

Children can recall when friends or siblings have shared something special with them, or helped them out when they have been feeling sad. They can recall experiences when they, too, have shared something in a special way. Class projects might include collecting toys for a poor family for the holidays or providing a meal for a family at Thanksgiving.

Hutchins, Pat. (1986). *The Doorbell Rang*. Greenwillow Books. P, 32 pages.

In *The Doorbell Rang*, two children who have a dozen cookies to share are happy until more and more children arrive at the house. They share until they are down to one cookie per child. When the doorbell rings once again, Mother suggests that they eat their cookies before answering it. But magnanimous Sam announces that he will open the door. Who is on the other side? It is Grandma, with a whole tray of cookies, and she is pleased to have so many people to share them with.

This story lends itself to a discussion about feelings. "How did the children feel about sharing the cookies and why?" "Was there any arguing? Why or why not?" "If the children wouldn't have shared, do you think the other children would want to continue coming to their house to play?" Children can act out the story, mainly as a math lesson in division, and at the end provide a tray of cookies. Linking math and social skills puts a new dimension upon learning (as does a tray of cookies!).

Children can draw pictures of a time when they have shared something with others. After completing the drawing, each child tells his or her story about this personal event and how it made people feel. It is from continual literary reinforcement and understanding peer feelings in various situations that a child can develop prosocial skills, such as sharing.

Keats, Ezra Jack. (1975). *Louie*. Greenwillow. P, I, 32 pages.

Louie, who has never been heard to talk, does so for the first time during a puppet show put on by some neighborhood children. He is obviously fascinated by the puppets, and especially one called Gussie. The rest of the children realize that he began to talk because of this fascination and see how badly Louie wants the puppet, so they give it to him.

Children can recall when they have really wanted something badly and write or tell about that experience. Did their wishes come true? Why or why not? As a follow-up, they can then take the part of donors and, putting themselves in their shoes, try to analyze how the donors knew they wanted the special thing.

Keats, Ezra Jack. (1972). *Pet Show*. Collier. P, 32 pages.

Archie wants to show his cat at the pet show, but his cat has run away. Reluctantly and creatively he adopts and enters a pet germ. A lady, who has found Archie's cat, enters him in the pet show, and Archie lets her keep the ribbon the cat wins.

In this story Archie has mixed feelings and, although sharing involves some sacrifice, he does it. Discussion of the story can focus on this aspect; it is an important and sometimes difficult step in children's moral growth.

Keenan, Martha. (1977). *The Mannerly Adventures of Little Mouse.* Illus. by Meri Shardin. Crown. P, 32 pages.

Little Mouse tries unsuccessfully to have good manners. When he finds a horde of food, however, he shares it with his entire family, thus demonstrating that there is more to manners than polite form.

This book might prompt a discussion of the roles of children in families. What do the children in the class contribute to their family's well-being? You might chart the chores the children have or other ways they are helpful at home. In a similar fashion children can help decide how to share responsibilities in the classroom. A discussion about manners and the underlying purpose for them can lead to an understanding of manners-related school rules. The discussion can then focus upon the thoughtfulness and mannerliness associated with some kinds of sharing.

Lobel, Anita. (1990). *Alison's Zinnia.* Lothrop, Lee & Shepard. P, I, 32 pages.

Girls whose names begin with each letter of the alphabet share a flower beginning with the same letter with another girl. Each child does something to give the flower to the next one.

Sharing flowers is one of the nicest ways for people to express friendship. A class that had a flower garden might find many opportunities to share their flowers. As a way to keep the flowers, children could learn how to press them.

Ravilious, Robin. (1991). *Two in a Pocket.* Little Brown. P, 32 pages.

Snippet, a dormouse, and Jenny Wren share a home together with Jenny sleeping during the night and Snippet during the day. Their daily habits can be annoying. If Snippet oversleeps, Jenny is flustered. If Snippet eats nuts in bed, Jenny becomes furious, and Jenny sings so loudly in the mornings that Snippet finds it hard to get to sleep. Yet they iron out their differences and become fast friends who depend upon each other.

Children often have to share bedrooms with their siblings and those who do will easily relate to the sharing that Snippet and Jenny Wren do. Even if they do not share bedrooms, children often have to share toys and, in school, they share limited resources. Dealing with each other's differences can be a challenge. Children can discuss and write about what makes sharing easy and what makes it difficult.

Roche, P. K. (1979). *Good-bye Arnold!* Dial. P, 32 pages.

Webster is at first delighted that his brother, Arnold, is going away for a week because now he won't have to share his possessions. As the week progresses, however, the joys of sharing become apparent and, when Arnold returns, both boys are far more unselfish than they ever have been before.

This book provides opportunities for thought, discussion, and writing on the topic of sharing with someone you care about. School can be a safe haven for children to share the joys and frustrations of having a sibling and to learn that others have similar experiences.

Shelby, Anne. (1991). *Potluck.* Illus. by Irene Trivas. Orchard. P, 32 pages.

Children whose names represent each letter of the alphabet bring an assortment of ethnic foods to a potluck supper.

Most children have experienced and enjoyed potluck meals where everyone shares their favorite recipes. A school follow-up activity would be to have a potluck luncheon in the classroom where small groups of children decide what to bring and prepare the foods together. Children often share foods from their lunch boxes (even when there are rules stating that they shouldn't), making food a useful entree into sharing other things.

Wagner, Jenny. (1977). *John Brown, Rose, and the Midnight Cat.* Illus. by Ron Brooks. Bradbury. P, I, 32 pages.

John Brown, a dog, does not want to share the affection and attention of his owner, Rose, with a stray cat that she invites into the house. By the end of the story John Brown changes his mind as jealousy is replaced by mutual respect.

Children who have pets and have special relationships with them can discuss the responsibilities of raising a pet and how these lead to feelings of loyalty. Some will have stories about the jealous behavior of a pet when a new one is brought home or when its owner pays attention to someone else. Sharing a friend can be difficult.

Wells, Rosemary. (1975). *Morris's Disappearing Bag.* Dial. P, 32 pages.

Morris's older brother and sister won't share their chemistry set or makeup kit which they received for Christmas. And they have no desire to play with Morris's stuffed toy. So Morris enters his "disappearing bag." All of a sudden the older siblings are very interested in sharing their presents with Morris so that they can have a turn with the disappearing bag.

Children can talk and write about what they can and cannot share with older or younger siblings or friends, and the reasons for those decisions. Just reasoning out why something should or not be shared, and with whom, helps children see various points of view. For example, they may easily identify with the older brother and sister who worry about the younger child's potential destructiveness, or with the younger child who feels left out.

Winthrop, Elizabeth. (1977). *That's Mine.* Illus. by Emily McCully. Holiday House. P, 32 pages.

A boy and girl argue over who should have control of the blocks and knock down each other's creations until they realize that by sharing the blocks they could build one big castle.

This book would be a good one to read early in the year to set the tone for cooperative learning and sharing of materials. After a brief discussion, you might take the children on a "tour" of the classroom in which you point out the materials that are in short supply, thus requiring cooperation and sharing. It would be to the children's benefit to plan for some materials to be limited, even if you have the option to supply plenty.

SUMMARY

The books on sharing deal predominantly with children who share toys or food and shelter. The toy sharing books include *Louie*; *Good-bye Arnold*; *I Sure Am Glad to See You, Blackboard Bear*; and *Dogger*. The books focusing upon the sharing of food or food and shelter, include *If You Give a Mouse a Cookie, The Mannerly Adventures of Little Mouse, One Fine Day, Twenty and Ten, Stone Soup, The Doorbell Rang, Potluck, Two in a Pocket,* and *The Grouchy Ladybug*. Jealousies that arise from pet attachment are addressed in *Pet Show, Cricket and the Crackerbox Kid,* and *John Brown, Rose, and the Midnight Cat*. In *Alison's Zinnia* girls share flowers. And in *The Clown of God* a man shares his talents.

Sharing appears to be done for several reasons—to meet a need, to distribute something, and for pleasure. Children tend to grow through discussions about why people in these stories share and whether the sharing is done equitably or not. Providing real opportunities for children to share makes them better understand the purposes for sharing.

CHAPTER 7

Truthfulness

RATIONALE

Stating the facts, presenting reality, behaving with honesty are what truthfulness is about. For very young children, even into the primary grades, these things may be difficult to achieve. They have a hard time sorting out fact from fiction, reality from fantasy. Often, in their minds, the two worlds blend, particularly when it is in their self-interest. For the youngest children this cannot usually be termed lying, because in their egocentrism and undeveloped sense of the world, it can make perfect sense to invent an answer that gets them what they think they need. They will even come to believe what they invented. Piaget called this "romancing" and observed, of course, that children grow out of it.

By first and second grade, children should have a better understanding of what is real and what isn't. (It is no accident that it is just about this time that virtually every child no longer accepts the reality of Santa Claus and the Easter Bunny.) From this point on and through the elementary years, teachers can profitably focus on fostering honesty in their children.

Why do children lie when we would prefer that they tell the truth? For the same reasons adults do: self-interest, self-preservation, and to retain power. Sometimes children feel pretty powerless, so they disobey an adult and do what they prefer; lying about what they have done may ensure that they keep their feeling of power. Or, they may not understand why an adult is asking them to do something and they resist doing it; lying about the situation helps them stay out of trouble for rebelling. Some will favor lying to being honest because of peer pressure. It is hard to stand up for what is right when one's peers are testing you.

You can structure a classroom or home environment to foster more truthfulness. Giving children a sense of power over their own lives and environment makes it less necessary for them to wrest power from you and later lie to you about what they are doing. Rather than seating children in rows, to work independently and in silence, use learning centers and cooperative learning. "Sharing with your neighbor" is then not a crime but a way to cooperate and be helpful. As a bonus, research is on the side of cooperative learning when it comes to high academic performance.

Make your classroom or home a safe place to tell the truth. Let children know that it's all right to make mistakes, to break things unintentionally, or to be angry now and then. Let them know that even adults make mistakes and can honestly talk about it when it happens.

Truthfulness was once more highly valued in our society than it now is. From our expectations that politicians will be dishonest to acceptance of rampant shoplifting and petty theft, we have come to assume that dishonesty is a part of American life. As parents and elementary teachers we can begin to reverse this trend. When we are open and honest with our children we model the kind of behavior we would like them to exhibit. When we trust them to take charge of their own learning and relationships with other children, our children will respond with more truthfulness.

As with the other moral issues covered in this book, there are some excellent children's books, mostly fiction stories, in which the ethic of truthfulness is embedded. These stories tend to be strong on plot as well as character development, and children can debate the issue of truthfulness and reflect upon reasons why the characters are not as truthful as they might be, and the consequences of their less than honest behavior.

CLASSROOM VIGNETTE

Elementary school children have a keen interest in honesty, particularly regarding the subject of stealing, an activity that is tempting to many. They need to learn about the issues involved and the attendant consequences. Linda found an unexpected opportunity to help children along these lines.

One day Linda was reading Megan McDonald's book, *The Potato Man* (Illus. by Ted Lewin, Orchard, 1991), to a group of third graders. In this book, Grandpa tells of an experience from his boyhood. It is the story of a one-eyed vegetable vendor who sold vegetables in Grandpa's neighborhood from a horse-pulled wagon. Grandpa and his friends taunted the potato man and when some potatoes bounced off the wagon, the boys hid them in their pockets and roasted them on a fire. They comment, "We shouldn'a taken these, it's like stealin'." Then around Christmas time, Grandpa's dog, Duke, finds a red pomegranate, which Grandpa recognizes as the Potato Man's. But when Grandpa tries to return it, the Potato Man tells him to keep it and wishes him a merry Christmas.

This story is rich with moral undertones. The children steal and know they should not have done that. As Linda was reading the book, the children stopped her when the boys took the potatoes and said, "They are stealing!" "They are gonna get caught!" In fact, the children did get caught and Grandpa had to peel potatoes for a whole week. Linda had chosen this book because the class was studying a vegetable theme for their science unit. The class made several kinds of potatoes from scratch after reading this book. They each got a turn with a potato peeler. But their first and most interested response to the story was concern about the boys stealing. The children talked about all the experiences they had seen, heard about, or participated in which involved stealing. Linda found it amazing to see how freely the children talked and their various encounters with this type of behavior. There was no doubt that these children knew that stealing was wrong, and that people's reasons for stealing involved rebellion, jealousy, and trying to get away with being sneaky.

A major question emerges at the end of the story. Why did the Potato Man give the pomegranate to the boy? These children said that he was an old man and could remember doing mischievous things as a child. He had been through a lot worse experiences (losing his eye) in the Great War. He needed Grandpa's friendship. There were a lot of responses to this question. These children's parents had all forgiven them for something and it made them feel very good. "That's how you know your mom loves you," one child said.

BOOK REVIEWS AND CURRICULAR EXTENSIONS

In the following bibliography, the grade-level designation "P" means the book might be more valuable in the primary grades, kindergarten to grade 3. The designation "I" means the intermediate grades 3-5.

Barracca, Debra & Barracca, Sal. (1991). *Maxi, the Hero.* Illus. by Mark Buehner. Dial. P, 32 pages.

Maxi the taxi dog and his partner Jim stop a thief from stealing a purse and become heros for their gallant efforts.

Unfortunately, purse-snatching and burglary are common events in the world today. Children can talk about what to do if they observe a crime and how to take precautions, such as locking doors and not wandering off by themselves. The humor in the book will generate light-hearted responses to the story as well. Children might relate this book to other dog hero books like the *Judge Benjamin, Superdog* (Minstrel) series and the series about *Carl* (Farrar, Strauss, & Giroux).

Brimmer, Larry Dane. (1990). *Cory Coleman, Grade 2.* Henry Holt. P, I, 68 pages.

Cory's best friend talks him into opening a hidden birthday present and trying it out. When it doesn't work, they are afraid they have broken it. An added problem arises when the class bully tries to ruin Cory's party at the skating rink. All ends well, as Mom realizes that Cory had opened the gift and gently teaches him a moral lesson about honesty. This is a short chapter book.

Children are tempted to do little dishonest things that on the surface don't amount to much, like opening a present before their birthday, "borrowing" something without asking, or doing something questionable if "nobody will find out." Yet from these little dishonest acts, larger moral issues arise. Children might talk about the minor situations that have tempted them and why they have or have not submitted to them. This book and *The Christmas Coat* by Clyde Robert Bulla both center around the theme of the consequences of dishonestly opening wrapped presents before a holiday.

Brown, Marc. (1983). *Arthur's April Fool.* Little, Brown. P, 32 pages.

Arthur, Buster, and Francine practice their magic tricks for the April Fool's Day assembly at school, but Arthur is afraid of Binky Barnes, the class bully, who has threatened to pulverize him. Arthur is so worried that he doesn't finish his supper and has nightmares the night before the assembly. When Binky responds to Arthur's invitation to volunteer for his magic tricks, Arthur is petrified. He summons all the courage he can and states that he plans to saw Binky in half. The trick works as Binky runs from the stage.

Children can discuss how the deception involved in April Fool's Day tricks is different from lying. Young children also need to examine the limits to which trickery can go and still remain a fun experience for everyone. And children who have been petrified of a class bully can tell how they overcame their fear.

Bulla, Clyde Robert. (1989). *The Christmas Coat.* Illus. by Sylvie Wickstrom. Alfred A. Knopf. P, I, 32 pages.

Two brothers open a gift their mother has hidden on the shelf of the closet, thinking that the gift is for them for Christmas. They argue about whose gift it is, damage the gift, and then have to work together to repair their damage.

Like Larry Dane Brimmer's *Cory Coleman, Grade 2*, the issue here is the dishonesty involved in invading people's privacy. Sneaking a look at a present may not be a large moral issue, but it is from small moral dilemmas that larger ones arise. Children can list, talk about, and role play temptations and debate the impact of their decisions at those times.

Carey, Valerie Scho. (1990). *Quail Song.* Illus. by Ivan Barnett. Putnam. P, 32 pages.

This retelling of a Pueblo Indian tale involves a quail who outwits a coyote. The quail cuts her foot on the sharp grass as she is winnowing, and cries out. Coyote hears her cry and, thinking it is a song, asks her to teach it to him. He doesn't listen to her when she tells him that it is not a song, but her crying, so she must pretend that she is singing in order to save her life from the coyote. Coyote keeps losing the song and returning to be taught again, until at last the quail sets up a rock decoy that looks just like she does. When coyote bites down on the rock, thinking it is the quail, he breaks a number of his teeth.

As with all trickster tales, children might discuss the difference between tricking and lying. Was justice done in this tale? Children might write about times when they have been tricked and how it made them feel or about times when they have tricked others. After letting them enjoy the power and humor that came from their success, ask them to imagine the feelings of the victim. Role play, in which the tricksters take the part of the victim, can be powerful if used with care. It is usually better to play out a story such as this than an actual situation, which is more threatening.

dePaola, Tomie. (1975). *Strega Nona.* Prentice-Hall. P, 32 pages.

Big Anthony, who comes to live with and help care for Strega Nona, is told not to touch the pasta pot, but after observing Strega Nona call upon its magical powers he cannot resist trying them out. Unfortunately, he didn't see Strega Nona blow three kisses to the magic pasta pot to stop the pot from producing pasta. One day Strega Nona leaves Big Anthony home while she goes over the mountain to the next town to visit a friend. Big Anthony successfully works the magic and the pot begins producing pasta, but he cannot make it stop. The pasta spreads over the streets and creates quite a mess. Not until Strega Nona returns from her visit is the spell broken. The townspeople, angry with Big Anthony, want to string him up, but Strega Nona insists that the punishment fit the crime and requires Big Anthony to eat all the pasta he made!

This is a wonderful story for discussing obedience. It is dishonest to disobey someone, especially after you have promised to be obedient. Children will have many disobedience tales to share. They can also explore the consequences of disobedience and determine whether they are logical or not. A chart might graph the "crime" and whether the consequence was logical or not. If the consequence was not logical the children could make up some that would have been.

deRegniers, Beatrice Schenk. (1985). *Jack and the Beanstalk.* Illus. by Anne Wilsdorf. Atheneum. P, I, 32 pages.

The tale of Jack and the Beanstalk involves Jack sneaking into the giant's home and stealing a hen that lays golden eggs, a singing harp, and a bag of money. This version, told in rhyme, rationalizes Jack's dishonesty by claiming that these riches originally belonged to Jack's father. When Jack first returns, his Mother explains, "I know this hen well. It belonged to your father.... the Giant took your father's hen, And he took your father's golden harp and all the gold that we had got." Jack's actions, then, are portrayed as justified to reclaim his family's belongings.

This version of the story might be compared with other versions, such as the one by John Howe, also reviewed in this chapter. Children might discuss how different ethics are sacrificed for the telling of a good story. Here the poor succeed over the rich, and the small over the large, even though they have to use trickery and deceit in order to triumph. Most children in the upper elementary grades are ready to learn that good and evil are not always easily defined. A book such as this makes understanding these differences easier.

Dinardo, Jeffrey. (1989). *The Wolf Who Cried Boy.* Putnam. P, 32 pages.

In this twist on the boy who cried wolf story, the moral of the story is the same: that when someone lies continually, people gradually stop listening to that person.

Many children have had experiences with individuals who have stretched the truth or asked for help when they didn't really need it. It is counter-productive to "cry wolf." There is a narrow line between tricking a friend and lying. One class suggested that it is tricking when both children laugh at the joke, and it is lying when one person feels bad about what the other one said. This story, and the original that inspired it, are excellent for role-play.

Harper, Wilhemina. (1967). *The Gunniwolf.* Dutton. P, 32 pages.

A mother leaves her daughter with the firm instructions not to go into the jungle next to her house, but once the mother departs, the little girl sees some beautiful flowers right at the edge of the jungle. After she picks those, she sees some more beautiful flowers just a bit further into the jungle. She keeps pursuing flowers until the Gunniwolf appears! Fortunately, the little girl escapes back home (though she must trick the Gunniwolf in order to do so). The effect of the moral emphasis on honesty and obedience is somewhat spoiled by the fact that the girl uses deception in her escape from the Gunniwolf.

The moral issue here is being dishonest or disobedient when temptations arise. Children might have a lively discussion about what tempts them. Would they do something bad or against the rules for money? How much? For toys, prizes, friendship? Children often hear, "If you do this, I'll be your friend." Since friendship is so very important to children, they are often tempted to do something dishonest to acquire a friend. Children need to be aware that they are being influenced and need to decide for themselves what is honest and dishonest behavior.

Harris, Joel Chandler. (1989). *Jump on Over! The Adventures of Brer Rabbit and His Family.* Adapted by Van Dyke Parks, Illus. by Barry Moser. Harcourt Brace Jovanovich. P, I, 44 pages.

Accompanied by beautiful water color and black-and-white full-page illustrations, 20 Brer Rabbit tales are told in very slight dialect, making for very easy oral reading.

These tales might be compared with the versions compiled by Julius Lester (described later in this chapter). Hearing two versions might make the theme of underdog in folktales come alive. Trickster tales are fun to analyze and children might debate whether the trick was ethically appropriate.

Herman, Charlotte. (1990). *Max Malone and the Great Cereal Rip-off.* Illus. by Catherine Smith. P, I, 59 pages.

Max is tired of getting ripped off by the advertisements on cereal boxes to send away for things. He writes a letter to one company complaining about a missing prize in a box of cereal. Later, at a garage sale, he has the opportunity to rip off a younger child who asks his advice about purchasing baseball cards. There is only one valuable card in the lot, and the child has selected it, though Max intended to buy it for himself. He ends up buying it for his friend.

This easy-to-read book for second and third graders is a lovely example of a realistic moral dilemma faced by children today. In the end Max makes a good decision, but the temptation to cheat was really strong. Children can talk and write about the times they have been tempted to be dishonest.

Howe, John. (1989). *Jack and the Beanstalk.* Little, Brown. P, 32 pages.

In this traditional telling of the tale, Jack trades his mother's last possession, a cow, for five bean seeds, which turn out to be magical and provide him with the means by which to climb to the giant's home and pilfer riches on which he and his mother can live for the rest of their lives.

Children might be asked to question Jack's stealing and relate it to the tales of Robin Hood and others who steal from the rich to care for the poor. This book is excellent for dramatization. At various turns of the plot, stop the role play and ask each character, in turn, how he or she feels.

Kellogg, Steven. (1991). *Jack and the Beanstalk.* Morrow. P, I, 48 pages.

In this traditional tale, Jack steals the ogre's property and escapes unscathed. The moral issues of the rich and the poor also come into play in this folktale. Children might debate whether it is ever right to steal and discuss the conditions that lead individuals to steal.

Kimmel, Eric. (1990). *Anansi and the Moss Covered Rock.* Holiday. P, 32 pages.

Anansi is the classic trickster. He tricks all the animals of the forest and steals their food, until at the end his dastardly deeds backfire. After attracting each one to look at the strange rock, where they are magically made unconscious when they speak the words, "I see a moss covered rock," Anansi rapidly returns to their home and steals their food. On the last trip to the rock, however, it is he who is outwitted, and while he is unconscious all of the animals retrieve their food. Children will enjoy this humorous, repetitive tale, and discussing the moral issues of stealing and tricking people won't detract from the overall story.

In one class the children talked about why it is important not to be tricked by other people, but to think on your own. This type of discussion can counter peer pressure to do things that are not right. Children can take Anansi's role and discuss the consequences to him of lying.

Lester, Julius. (1987). *The Tales of Uncle Remus: The Adventures of Brer Rabbit.* Illus. by Jerry Pinkney. Dial. P, I, 128 pages.

Lester, Julius. (1988). *More Tales of Uncle Remus: Further Adventures of Brer Rabbit, His Friends, Enemies, and Others.* Illus. by Jerry Pinkney. Dial. P, I, 128 pages.

Brer Rabbit is not as big as Brer Bear; nor are his teeth and claws as sharp as Brer Fox; but Brer Rabbit can outwit them both in these humorous tales of the American South. The second book introduces new characters such as Brer Bullfrog and Brer Alligator.

Trickster tales are not moral because the trickster lies, cheats, and deceives and the reward for his trickery is not punishment, but victory. The trickster's vitality is more important to the tale than right or wrong. Children can relate to these tales because they typically know a trickster—a class clown who always seems to be up to something. They can discuss times when tricking is morally defensible and times when it is not.

Lowry, Lois. (1991). *Anastasia at this Address.* Houghton Mifflin. I, 112 pages.

Anastasia, an inveterate letter-writer, answers an advertisement in the paper to correspond with a "SWM, 28, boyish charm, inherited wealth." While Anastasia hasn't exactly *lied* to her pen pal, she hasn't told him all of the truth either, and panics when he announces that he is coming for a visit.

All children have stretched the truth at one time or another and will have stories to tell about what happened and the importance of honesty. Children can also recall times when they have experienced the results of little white lies.

Mayer, Mercer. (1976). *Liza Lou and the Yeller Belly Swamp.* Four Winds. P, 32 pages.

Liza Lou has errands to run for her Momma which entail traveling through the swamp. In the swamp she encounters a pale, nasty swamp haunt, a swamp witch, and a gobblygook, but she outwits each of them. Here trickery is essential for Liza Lou's survival.

Sharing books like these with young children helps them determine the difference between fact and fiction. Tricking (lying) is fun in fantasy stories, but it would not be appropriate in real life.

Ness, Eveline. (1966). *Sam, Bangs & Moonshine.* Holt, Rinehart and Winston. P, I, 32 pages.

Samantha, called Sam for short, had the reckless habit of lying, or more accurately, fantasizing. She called her mother a mermaid and her cat, Bangs, a lion. Her parents urge her to talk real, not moonshine, but that is impossible for Sam. Sam engages her young friend Thomas in very fanciful play, and because he believes everything Sam says, he participates fully in her adventures. One day, Sam sends Thomas on a search for a baby kangaroo. She is terrified when neither he nor Bangs returns and a dreadful storm threatens to raise the tide to cover the rock where Thomas was headed. Sam's father rescues Thomas, but not Bangs. Bangs does return later, however.

The lesson here is to differentiate between fact and fantasy, something young children must be able to do as they progress toward understanding honesty. Children can recall their fantasy play. Some will be able to identify times when they were so engrossed in their play that they disregarded reality.

Scieszka, Jon. (1989). *The True Story of the 3 Little Pigs! By A. Wolf.* Illus. by Lane Smith. Viking Kestral. P, I, 32 pages.

A. Wolf claims that he was framed and that he is not such a big bad wolf after all. In his version of the three little pigs story, he was seeking a cup of sugar from a neighbor in order to bake a birthday cake for his dear old granny. His neighbor turned out to be one of the pigs, and a sneeze from his cold demolished the house and, unfortunately, the pig. He only ate the pig so as to not waste food.

This hilarious book is a great way to start a discussion of looking at things from different perspectives. Truthfulness often depends upon the angle from which you are viewing a situation. Children can talk about times when it looked like one thing happened, but in reality it was another. They can have fun rewriting folk and fairy tales from the point of view of the perpetrator of harm.

Spinelli, Jerry. (1991). *Fourth Grade Rats.* Scholastic. I, 128 pages.

Fourth-grader Suds has to decide between doing what is right and joining the Rats. In an effort to be grown up and gain the approval of the gang, Suds throws away his teddy bear and lets a bee crawl up his arm. These actions impress a girl he likes, but increasingly he is morally uncomfortable with the antics of this peer group.

Most upper elementary children have experienced a keen desire for belonging to a group. They can talk about how it feels to join in on activities they don't really like, just for the approval of the group. They might also talk about how it feels to stand up for one's beliefs even if they are not popular with a group.

Stevens, Kathleen. (1982). *Molly, McCullough, & Tom the Rogue*. Illus. by Margot Zemach. Thomas Y. Crowell. P, I, 32 pages.

A rogue named Tom Devlin makes his living by his wits. He takes his horse and cart up to a village inn, and inquires as to who is the richest farmer in the region. He tricks that rich farmer into selling him a bit of land and then drops a fake map which indicates that the land the farmer has just sold is rich with treasure. When the farmer tries to renege on the deal, the rogue threatens to ruin his reputation in the town. The farmer gets his money back and the rogue returns his land only after the farmer has given him something to "soften the loss," which Tom exchanges at the local market for money. Tom is finally outwitted by a feisty young lady named Molly who substitutes straw for cabbages as his bounty. In the end they drive off together.

There is one point in children's moral development when justice is served by doing to the perpetrator of evil exactly what he has done to you. Such is the case with this story, and children who are at that level will agree that dishonesty has been rightfully punished by more dishonesty. Children who are more mature will recognize the classic trickster tale as a fictional tale, and can discuss its moral at a more complex level.

Stevenson, James. (1991). *That's Exactly the Way It Wasn't*. Greenwillow. P, I, 32 pages.

In one of a series of stories illustrated in cartoon fashion, two grandfathers who are brothers reminisce about their youth. In this book, the men can't agree about anything that happened. Each keeps correcting the other until they finally agree about enjoying some ice cream.

Interesting discussions will evolve about unintentional lying and the difficulty of recalling exactly what happened to get at the underlying truth of two conflicting stories. Sometimes children are not lying when conflicts arise. They simply can't recall the truth or there are two different perspectives on what really is the truth. When there is a conflict in the classroom, have the two children sit down next to each other (one teacher had a learning center for this activity) and have them write out what caused the difficulty and their ideas for a solution. It will surprise the children when they read the other's perspective on why there was a conflict. Have the children sit and plan together until they have worked out a harmonious solution.

SUMMARY

It's important to realize that how we act, think, and feel can affect those around us.

Truthfulness is a value that must be taught and encouraged while children are young because competition in school and the workplace can produce a great deal of stress. If this value is not taught when children are young, the pressures inculcated by school, friends, and the workplace may cause some people to be dishonest: to cheat, lie, steal, or be unfair. These behaviors, in the long run, will ruin a person's integrity and ability to function in our society.

The books reviewed on the topic of truthfulness tended to deal with five related issues: stealing, trickery, obedience, cheating, and lying. Each of these subtopics lends itself to different strategies for helping children acquire a deeper understanding of the ethic of truthfulness. *Maxi, the Hero* involves a man and a dog intervening and stopping a purse-snatcher. Stealing surfaces as an issue faced by a child in *The Potato Man* and is evidenced, though not discussed, in the many versions of *Jack and the Beanstalk*. Young children can learn that sneaking or taking something that doesn't belong to you is wrong. As they become involved with dividing toys and resources, they learn not to take something that does not belong to them. Older children can deal with more complex issues of why people steal and the difference between stealing as presented in a realistic fiction book and stealing in a folktale. Is it ever justifiable to steal from the rich and give to the poor?

Trickster tales can involve tricking to save one's life, as in *Quail Song* and *Liza Lou and the Yeller Belly Swamp,* or tricking as a way of obtaining food or one's livelihood, as in *Anansi and the Moss Covered Rock* and *Molly, McCullough, & Tom the Rogue*. Some trickster tales have no moral ethic whatsoever, such as the Uncle Remus tales. These provide a springboard for discussion about the issue of tricking others, however. Young children can enjoy simple trickster tales and playing tricks, while at the same time learning to be sensitive about hurting each other's feelings. Older children might enjoy a whole unit on trickster tales in literature and might enjoy predicting how the perpetrator of the tricks would get his or her comeuppance. In American culture, April Fool's Day is set aside for the playing of tricks on one another. *Arthur's April Fool* not only helps children prepare for that day, but also provides support for children to outwit the "bad guys" and bullies.

Related to trickery and honesty is the ability to cheat someone. Cheating is the theme of *Max Malone and the Great Cereal Rip-off*. Lying is a theme of the humorous, *Anastasia at this Address,* because Anastasia corresponds with an older man without telling him that she is just 15 years old! Upper elementary children often struggle with the issue of peer pressure, especially when the peer group advocates something that the individual thinks is wrong, as in *Fourth Grade Rats*.

Obedience is based upon truthfulness. To disobey is dishonest. Consequences for disobedience are shown in *Strega Nona* and *The Gunniwolf*. Two books center around problems that arise when children disobediently open wrapped presents that are hidden in the house (*Cory Coleman, Grade 2* and *The Christmas Coat*). Lying or stretching the truth also have bad effects. *The Wolf Who Cried Boy* has carried trickery too far and can get no one to respond to him. *Sam, Bangs and Moonshine* is a more serious treatment of the topic of telling the truth and distinguishing between fact and fantasy. Noticing that the truth depends upon one's perspective is the focus of *The True Story of the 3 Little Pigs* and *That's Exactly the Way It Wasn't*. Whether humorous or serious, whether fantasy or realistic, these books share with children some of the reasons to be honest and trustworthy and the fact that dishonesty has its consequences.

CHAPTER 8

Solving Conflicts Peacefully

RATIONALE

The first steps toward world peace begin in our interactions with each other. Children can understand this and learn how to solve little problems as well as big ones in nonviolent ways. So often when conflicts occur between children in school, they resort to hitting or name-calling as solutions. Getting them to stop and think first, to be aware of alternatives and to have the self-control needed to select from among these alternatives makes peacemakers out of the very children who would most likely become violent. We can't assume that children arrive at school knowing how to behave kindly towards each other any more than we can assume they arrive at school knowing how to read and write. Children must learn how to behave in a group so that their interactions with others are positive.

Conflict between children arises for many of the same reasons it arises between adults. Territorial expansion has caused wars since the beginning of time, and children, wanting to expand their area of play, can thoughtlessly ruin the play of others who are in their way. Conflict can arise, too, when one country wants access to another's resources; children can grow impatient to use classroom materials that are in short supply. The conflicts that come from differing values tear apart marriages, political parties, churches, and even countries. For children in classrooms, value conflicts also emerge. For example, a child may want to report another who has been stealing, but a friend convinces the child that tattling is worse. Perhaps the child who stole did it to win popularity with a group of potential friends, deciding that friendship is a greater value than honesty.

The adjustment from a home environment to school is a bigger one than is recognized by many adults. Children go from being the center of attention to being only one of a large group. Jealousies arise. Children want and need individual attention. They need to feel wanted and needed both at home and at school. Sometimes children boast and brag as a way of covering up their true feelings. Boastful behavior is in no way endearing and causes more problems than it solves.

Children need a variety of strategies to cope with conflict, and a good many books are available that suggest good alternatives. In children's books, conflicts and disagreements often occur as part of the plot. A book can be read aloud to the point of the conflict and children can be encouraged to predict what will happen and how the problem will be solved. They can compare their ideas with those of the author.

CLASSROOM VIGNETTE

Some books provide a springboard to class discussion and role-play situations which help children focus upon the moral of the story. In the following example, Kathy found that although children could talk about ways to solve problems peacefully, they couldn't put their words into action until they thoughtfully reflected upon a book, practiced their responses through role-play, and then made charts to remind them of what they had learned.

The Hating Book, by Charlotte Zolotow (Harper, 1969) serves as a perfect introduction to learning how to solve conflicts peacefully. Kathy wrote a class chart prior to reading the book; the chart was titled, "Ways to solve a problem peacefully." She was surprised that her first graders knew how to solve a problem peacefully. Their list included: "Talk it out." "Say, 'Stop! That makes me feel bad.'" "Ignore the other person." "Walk away." "Talk to an adult."

Interestingly, the children had not entered into a developmental stage in which they could use this information in a real life situation unless there was constant reinforcement with literature and role playing.

As an introduction to *The Hating Book,* Kathy showed the class the front cover. Two children in a boxing stance are depicted, each wearing a mask with an angry face. She asked the class why they thought the illustrator put masks on the children. One child replied, "Maybe they feel like that on the outside, but not really. I think they really like each other."

This story lends itself to a shared reading experience where the children read or chant along with the adult who is reading aloud. In this case, the repeated phrase the children read was, "I hate, hate, hated my friend." Two pages of the book have no words, just a picture showing one of the girls knocking on the door at her friend's house. Kathy asked the class at this point to guess what the girl was going to say to her friend. They referred back to the chart they had created prior to reading the story and noticed that they had listed, "talk it out," as one of their ideas. This revelation impressed the class. After reading the book, Kathy encouraged high level literature responses by asking the children, "When did you have a problem with a friend and you worked it out by talking?" or "Was there ever a time you had a fight with a friend that you could have worked out peacefully by talking?"

Kathy asked the class to share some of the problems they had experienced. Pushing, hitting, name calling, and not sharing are important issues in the primary years and these were all mentioned. The children then practiced role playing, using their chart to remind them of ways to work out difficult situations. The rest of the class became the audience, offering helpful suggestions on different ways to work out each problem. Kathy's approach can be a valuable tool to use when real problems do occur. The teacher is taken out of the role as a disciplinarian and put in the role of facilitating moral values.

The next day the class reviewed their role playing and made a new chart: "Choices I can make if I am angry." The children came up with positive alternatives to hitting and name calling. This served as a reminder when they were tempted to make inappropriate choices.

BOOK REVIEWS AND CURRICULAR EXTENSIONS

In the following bibliography, the grade-level designation "P" mans the book might be more valuable for the primary grades, kindergarten to grade 3. The designation "I" means the intermediate grades 3-5.

Baker, Keith. (1990). *Who Is the Beast?* Harcourt Brace Jovanovich. P, 32 pages.

In a rhyming chant, a tiger looks around him and finds many other animals with stripes, tails, green eyes, and other qualities that he does not recognize as his own until he looks into a pond and sees his reflection. He finally discovers that there is no need for alarm because each "beast" he sees has something in common with him.

Children can discuss bullies and how to deal with them. They can share how solving conflicts takes more courage than physical strength. Even though individuals are different in appearance, inside they all share many of the same internal qualities.

Brown, Ruth. (1990). *I Don't Like It*. Dutton. P, 32 pages.

The heroine of this story is a doll who has always been the favorite possession of her owner. The doll is upset and jealous when a new puppy arrives on the scene and steals all of the little girl's attention. She asks each of her toy friends what he or she thinks about the new puppy, but they aren't jealous as she is. One day the puppy grabs the doll and hides her under a chest of drawers, and the little girl refuses to go to sleep without her. Then the doll knows how very special she actually is. When she is eventually found, all is well once more.

Most children can recognize feelings of jealousy. They are jealous of their siblings and of their friends, and even of their pets if they feel they're getting too much attention. They can talk and write about times when they felt jealous and how they handled those feelings. More effective handling of such feelings can be promoted by some extended discussion.

Bulla, Clyde Robert. (1989). *The Christmas Coat.* Illus. by Sylvie Wickstrom. Alfred A. Knopf. P, I, 32 pages.

Two brothers argue and bicker continuously. Their mother doesn't know what to do because she has to work and the boys are home alone, constantly quarreling and fighting. In desperation, the mother draws a chalk line down the center of the room and requires each boy to stay on his own side of the line. The boys continue to bicker. Three days before Christmas the boys open a box they should not have touched and end up tearing a coat that does not even belong to them or their mother. They quickly learn to cooperate, take the coat to a tailor, and have it mended in time for their mother's friend to give it to her son for Christmas. The coat will allow this poor child to play outside in the snow. It makes the brothers happy to have cooperated so that the boy can have a coat that means so very much to him. As the two brothers move from an intense rivalry into problem solving skills, the result is honesty, fairness, and the boys' realization that their actions do affect others.

Two elements of literature are characterization and plot development. Literature responses and internalization of values are at a higher level when they relate to children's lives. *The Christmas Coat* provides the perfect stage for following character and plot development. You can create a "feelings graph" to plot the feelings of the boys and the mother as the story progresses. Children will visually see how the boys feel better when they cooperate than when they are bickering with each other. More important, they will realize that the boys' actions affect the mother's feelings. She, too, feels better when they are cooperative and responsible. Children can then recall times when their actions might have affected how their parents or others felt.

Cole, Brock. (1986). *The Giant's Toe.* Farrar, Straus and Giroux. P, I, 32 pages.

In a parody of Jack and the Beanstalk, the giant accidentally chops off his toe, which becomes a tiny boy. The giant tries to get rid of the toe by baking him in a pie, but the boy changes places with the hen that lays the golden eggs, and the giant bakes the hen in a pie instead. The giant is understandably angry and vows to get rid of the toe. In the end they make peace. This is an extremely funny story in both illustration and text.

The issue here is what to do when you are angry. Yelling and threatening don't work well. The toe's patient, calm, helpful demeanor wins out in the end. The humor in this story can be used as a running joke in class. Does a child become unreasonably angry? Offer to chop off his or her toe so a peacemaker will be available!

Durrell, Ann & Sachs, Marilyn (Eds.). (1990). *The Big Book of PEACE.* Dutton. I, 54 pages.

This collection of original short stories and poetry, written by some of the foremost authors of children's literature and illustrated by some of the most talented illustrators, is a celebration of peacemaking. The proceeds from the sale of the book go to several peace organizations. There are some poignant stories here to share with all ages of children. Many topics are covered, such as homelessness, war, and arguments.

Children might write their own peace stories, based on positive classroom experiences. These can be collected and bound as a way to celebrate their efforts to be caring, calm, and considerate citizens of the classroom.

Golenboch, Peter. (1990). *Teammates.* Gulliver/Harcourt Brace Jovanovich. P, I, 32 pages.

Teammates chronicles Jackie Robinson's experience as the first Black baseball player to play on a major league team. Jackie was extremely calm and peaceful in the face of other people's anxieties on that day. The whole picture book biography highlights Jackie as a peacemaker.

Because this book is a true story about a real person who was peaceful and yet made history for his actions, it is a very powerful book for children. They might discuss and write about the real people they know in their own community who are or have been peacemakers in tense situations.

Haviland, Virginia. (1990). *The Talking Pot.* Illus. by Melissa Sweet. Little, Brown. P, 32 pages.

A very poor man trades his last possession, a cow, for a talking pot in this Danish folktale. As in Jack and the Beanstalk, the woman is outraged at the horrible trade the man had made, scolding and abusing her husband. "You are a great blockhead!" she tells him. The pot, however, takes off for the rich man's house where it steals food, grain, and money for the poor man. The poor man makes sure to point out to his wife that the bargain was an excellent one after all, and she agrees.

The name-calling is not the main point of this story, but it is prominent for children to notice. As with the other name-calling books, children can seek alternatives to that type of behavior, which does nothing to solve the conflict.

Hedderwick, Mairi. (1986). *Katie Morag and the Tiresome Ted.* Little, Brown. P, 32 pages.

Katie is jealous of all the attention being given to a new baby in the family. At one point she becomes so angry that she throws her beloved teddy into the ocean. That night she regrets her decision. Her resentful behavior and a wet bed in the morning cause her parents to send her to her grandmother's on the other end of the island for a few days. There, her teddy is washed up on shore. She restuffs it and mends it, borrowing a sleeper from the baby to cover up the repair work. She thoughtfully brings something from the beach home for each member of her family. One assumes that Katie has learned not to lose her temper quite so easily and she definitely exhibits responsible behavior in repairing her teddy on her own.

Children might recall times when they have lost their tempers and the results of that behavior. They might brainstorm a chart as Kathy's class did on "What to do when you are angry." When you want to hit, call names, or throw something, what other ways are there to relieve the anger, and yet not be destructive or hurt someone physically or mentally?

Johansen, Hanna. (1991). *The Duck and the Owl.* Illus. by Kathi Bhend. Dutton. P, 32 pages.

Owl and Duck are best friends even though they are very different from each other. Duck sleeps at night while Owl sleeps during the day. Duck lives near a pond while Owl lives in a tree. In spite of their differences, or because of them, the two become fast friends—yet they engage in many foolish squabbles. Their secret desire to become friends helps them understand each other's peculiar habits and ways.

Children will recall the many silly arguments they have had with their siblings and friends. They might make a list of these squabbles and think about how they might have been avoided and how they were solved. They might role-play these problems and have classmates suggest solutions. The more they practice solving little problems peacefully, the easier it becomes to handle larger problems when they arise.

Jones, Rebecca C. (1991). *Matthew and Tillie.* Illus. by Bess Peck. Dutton. P, I, 32 pages.

Tillie is Black and Matthew is White and they are best friends. After a fight, they decide to separate, but once on their own, they find out that they are lonely and miss each other. Play is not much fun without a best friend, so they get back together.

A class might chart things it is fun to do with a friend. They might analyze all the reasons that friends have conflicts and discuss how they might deal with those problems. They might also discuss feelings of loneliness and how to combat those feelings. Noticing that the main characters are of different races, the children can talk about their friends who are racially different. If the class is all of one race, discussions on this topic will be no problem. If the class has children from different races who work and play well together, they will take for granted that people from different races can be best friends and no discussion is needed. If, on the other hand, the children in a racially mixed class are having difficulty solving problems peacefully, sensitive discussions on the topic focusing around a book instead of their real lives may serve as a catalyst for healing racial tensions. The teacher might purposely give the children the opportunity to select someone from a different race to play with during free play time. In upper elementary grades children can even discuss how you solve problems differently with people of different cultures and different relationships. You certainly solve problems differently with a best friend and with a stranger, or with a parent and a friend.

Keats, Ezra Jack. (1967). *Peter's Chair.* Harper. P, 32 pages.

Peter becomes very jealous when his little chair gets painted pink for his new baby sister. He decides to run away with a few of his most precious belongings. He only gets as far as the front of the house before he comes to terms with his jealous feelings and returns home.

Children can talk about the disruptions to the family caused by new babies and how to adjust to those disruptions. They may want to share experiences in which their own jealous feelings prompted them to create conflict. Away from home, it may be easier to discuss their feelings and think of more peaceful solutions.

Kellogg, Stephen. (1973). *The Island of the Skog.* Dial. P, 32 pages.

The mice set sail for a safer place to live, free from cats, and arrive on an island they believe to be uninhabited, only to find that a skog lives there. No one has seen the skog, but the evidence indicates that it is a huge nocturnal animal. This is a clear case of jumping to conclusions without enough evidence, and an example of how threatening one's enemy does not work. In the end, the skog turns out to be a shy little animal who was afraid of the mice.

Children can recall times when they jumped to unfounded conclusions. In school someone is always stating, "Somebody stole my pencil," when nine times out of ten the pencil fell to the floor and remains there. Children might also talk and write about their fears.

Ravilious, Robin. (1991). *Two in a Pocket.* Little, Brown. P, 32 pages.

Snippet, a dormouse, and Jenny Wren are in conflict because they both want to live in the same home, a nest in the pocket of an old jacket hanging in the barn. Jenny Wren calls Snippet names: "Thief! Burglar! Pickpocket!" and orders the dormouse out of her nest. When the dormouse explains that it was a cat that chased her into the nest, the two talk over their problem and decide to share the home. They become fast friends, and later in the story Snippet ends up saving Jenny's life.

Children can talk about the times conflict arose because they wanted something someone else had—or someone else wanted what they had. At home conflict can arise when two people want to watch television shows at the same time; or one wants the light out but the other wants to stay up and read. Solving conflicts like these is challenging. Children could role-play this story and other problems they have sharing with their siblings and friends.

Sharmat, Marjorie. (1975). *I'm Not Oscar's Friend Anymore.* Illus. by Tony DeLuna. Dutton. P, 32 pages.

Anger causes the hero of this story to recite a long list of evil afflictions that his friend Oscar deserves, but in the end he decides to give Oscar one more chance to apologize. Oscar can't even remember the event that led to the conflict!

This story models two good solutions to argument—giving someone another chance and making an apology. Children will relate to the humor of not remembering what started the argument in the beginning and be able to recount their own experiences with short-lived fights with friends.

Smalls-Hector, Irene. (1991). *Irene and the Big, Fine Nickel.* Illus. by Tyronne Geter. Little, Brown. P, 32 pages.

Harlem in 1957 is the setting for *Irene and the Big, Fine Nickel.* In those days Harlem was like a southern Black community where you were "surrounded by a million people who looked just like you," and no one locked doors. Seven-year-old Irene and Charlotte play together in the story, which has little plot, but merely records their many activities. At one point, however, they get into an argument and one child yells, "mamma" at the other. Nothing triggers resentment and anger like that word! Irene greases her body in preparation for their big fight, but conflict is avoided when they find a nickel and decide together to spend it on a raisin bun to share.

Children might list words that really make them angry and then discuss name-calling and how to avoid it or handle it when it occurs. Cultural and sexual differences as well as individual differences might surface as different terms offend different groups of children. Children might then make a chart of alternative things to say when they are angry with one another.

Thayer, Jane. (1953/1989). *The Popcorn Dragon.* Illus. by Lisa McGue. Morrow. P, 32 pages.

Dragon is a little showoff, blowing smoke and acting in an inconsiderate manner for a dragon. He loses friends and feels lonely. When he finds himself in a corn field and is able to use his hot air to pop popcorn for his friends, he explains to them that he has learned that he shouldn't be a showoff.

Children can relate to times when a child's showing off has hindered their feelings of friendship. They can also reflect back upon times when they have shown off and discuss the results of that behavior. In analyzing causes of conflict among friends, showing off often surfaces, and children need to learn that their behaviors affect others.

Turkle, Brinton. (1978). *Rachel and Obadiah.* Dutton. P, 32 pages.

Rachel and Obadiah, a Quaker sister and brother who live on Nantucket Island in the early 1800s, have a conflict. Each wants to be chosen to run the message from the mill to the captain's wife when a sailing ship arrives at Nantucket Harbor. They solve their conflict by having a running race, with Obadiah letting Rachel start first because she is the youngest. When Obadiah shows off by running in circles around Rachel and by stopping to pick blackberries, Rachel continues on and wins the race. She receives two silver coins for delivering the news. The last page shows Rachel with the two coins in her hand and Obadiah arriving, blackberry juice trickling down his chin. What will she do with *two* coins?

Children can discuss and write about the times when they have had conflicts with their brothers and sisters or friends, telling how they solved or might have solved their conflicts peacefully. Issues of fairness and equality arise. Should sisters and brothers be treated equally? Does fair and equal treatment mean that Rachel should have started the race at the same time as Obadiah did? Is being equal the only way parents or teachers can be fair?

Waber, Bernard. (1988). *Ira Says Goodbye.* Houghton Mifflin. P, 32 pages.

From the look on his face on the dust jacket of the book, you can tell that Ira and his best friend Reggie have had an argument. Reggie is about to move away and not only do the boys have to distribute their jointly owned possessions, but also Ira is jealous because his friend seems happy to be moving away from him. The argument ends in a generous and friendly decision by Ira to keep their pet turtles together. Ira learns that he and Reggie can still be friends, even at long distance.

So often it is possessions over which children argue. Dividing up treasures can be difficult. Children reading this book will recall times when they felt that their friends were unjust in the distribution of items they had shared. Often the issue of "lending" as opposed to "giving" things to each other surfaces. Interesting discussions could clarify definitions of terms and help children mature in their outlook about sharing toys and possessions with friends.

Winthrop, Elizabeth. (1983). *Katharine's Doll.* Illus. by Marylin Hafner. Dutton. P, 32 pages.

Molly is Katharine's best friend, so when Katharine receives a beautiful doll from her grandmother, they both play with it every day. Finally, jealousy overcomes Katharine, who accuses Molly of coming to play with her doll instead of her! The girls argue and are no longer friends, until Katharine realizes that there are many things she can do with her friend that she can't do alone with her doll.

Children might discuss times when a favorite toy has come between them and a friend or when jealousy over a toy has caused a rift in their relationships. They might create a list of all of the things they like to do alone and all of the things they like to do with friends to realize how important friends are to them. If a relationship is important, it takes effort to help it grow. Children can discuss how they work to avoid conflicts over possessions in their friendships.

SUMMARY

Children will face conflicts in their lives. They need to know how to handle them peacefully. Feelings like jealousy surface when children must adjust to new babies in the family (*Katie Morag and the Tiresome Ted* and *Peter's Chair*), when there is sibling rivalry (*Rachel and Obadiah*), and when friends quarrel over toys and possessions (*Ira Says Goodbye*, *Katharine's Doll*, and *I Don't Like It*). Children can learn how to deal with jealous feelings by comparing how these story characters overcame those feelings.

Anger is another feeling that surfaces both at home and at school. *The Hating Book* and *The Giant's Toe* are two good books which address ways to deal with anger. One way often used by children to deal with anger is name-calling. In *Two in a Pocket*, *The Talking Pot*, and *Irene's Big, Fine Nickel*, story characters react to name-calling and conflicts are avoided. Role-playing is an excellent strategy for practicing strategies for dealing with anger.

Sometimes conflicts are caused by children bullying each other, or by children's fears of children they don't know well, whom they perceive as bullies. *The Beast* and *The Island of the Skog* treat the issue of getting a clearer perception of people who appear to be bullies. Larger conflicts such as war are addressed in *The Big Book of PEACE* and *Teammates*. These and the bully issue are best handled through classroom discussions.

Often conflicts arise through petty bickering at home among siblings (*The Christmas Coat*) or among friends (*I'm Not Oscar's Friend Anymore*, *The Duck and the Owl*, and *Matthew and Tillie*). Bragging is also sometimes a source of conflict, as in *The Popcorn Dragon*.

Children need to learn how to stop fighting, bickering, and complaining in order to have joyous school experiences. Discussion and role-play of events with the potential for conflict provide the best teaching strategies for helping children analyze their antagonistic feelings and deal with them.

CHAPTER 9

Respecting and Appreciating Others

RATIONALE

Children learn to value themselves when they value other people. When they respect and appreciate what is good and special in others, they need not feel defensive or competitive about their own unique traits and ideas. They come to know that everyone, including themselves, deserves the regard of others. They cooperate and are helpful to one another without being asked.

In the United States there has been a long history of valuing conformity in the face of increasing diversity. American culture often promotes conformity. For example, advertising slogans use the bandwagon approach, urging us to do as our peers allegedly are doing. Yet, in a democratic society such as ours, it is important that children learn to stand on their own two feet and make intelligent life decisions based on more than peer pressure.

One situation in which this need is greatest concerns the respect and appreciation of others. As the populace of our country becomes increasingly diverse, it becomes ever more important that children value others for their positive qualities and not because they conform to some prejudiced model.

American classrooms can be set up democratically, providing opportunities for children to respect each other's property and rights. Children can learn to care for classroom materials and resources. Providing neatly labeled and organized storage spaces tells children that the equipment and materials in their classroom are valued. Children need classroom responsibilities allowing them to take care of class pets, clean the room, and turn out the lights. When children take responsibility for their classroom, they learn to be cooperative team players who care for others in the classroom community.

Many children's books focus on these concepts. They help us love and appreciate those who are different; they provide examples of respect for others and rules; and they show positive caring behaviors toward those who are different. In fact, multicultural children's literature is flourishing during the 1990s. Realistic stories, folktales, and nonfiction from many different cultures are being published. Every time children read or hear about people in cultures different from their own, the experience becomes more common and accepted. Discussing the humane elements of the stories and using them as models of caring behavior helps children acquire this special aspect of moral development.

Children can develop empathy for story characters and their varying situations through literature, role playing, and journal writing. Empathy is an important step in developing kindness and respect for others. Children's literature is full of examples of such attitudes and related behavior on the part of book characters. Realistic fiction books relate to the child's every day life and provide wonderful models for discussion, opportunities for high level responses to literature, and lead toward the internalization of moral values.

Respect and appreciation for others is critical at this time in our history. If our nation is truly going to end prejudiced actions against those who are different, we must raise a generation of children who see other people's differences as an asset, not a handicap.

CLASSROOM VIGNETTE

Children often are enticed by peer pressure or insecurity into laughing at others. Here is a book that aided one class in dealing with the problem, and it did so through silly humor.

The Cow that Went OINK by Bernard Most (Harcourt Brace Jovanovich, 1990) is a simple picture book that has value at all elementary grade levels. While levels of response will be higher in older children, the moral issue of making fun of others who are different remains an issue for all ages. All the cows on the farm laughed at the cow that went "Oink." All the pigs on the farm laughed at the pig that went "Mooo." The other animals on the farm laughed at them also. This made the cow and the pig very sad. Instead of being mean to the other animals on the farm, the cow and the pig decided to help each other by teaching each other the appropriate sounds. Imagine the feeling each of them had as they became the only bilingual animals on the farm!

This book provides an excellent reference for children who recall when they laughed at someone who was different or they themselves were laughed at. Toni's second grade class noticed how the pig and cow ignored the taunts of the other animals. "Mrs. Aguirre, that's what you told us to do on the playground!" said Danny. "Yeah, and I never thought it would work," commented Jose.

Toni then asked, "Is there anything else we can learn from this story?" At the moment, the children were so interested in their first observation that they had nothing to add. A few days later, the children requested a repeat reading of the popular story. This time, one of the boys had an answer: "I think this book is really about people who can do special things. And we should be nice to them even if the things are kinda funny." The children then held an impromptu demonstration of their various musical and gymnastic talents and everyone applauded every act.

Books like *The Cow that Went OINK* fit right into a classroom curriculum that focuses positively on children's unique characteristics and talents. It serves as a model in developing respect for others.

BOOK REVIEWS AND CURRICULAR EXTENSIONS

In the following bibliography, the grade-level designation "P" means the book might be more valuable for the primary grades, kindergarten to grade 3. The designation "I" means the intermediate grades 3-5.

Anholt, Lawrence. (1991). *What I Like*. Illus. by Catherine Anholt. Putnam. P, 32 pages.

Six different children share what they like doing in a simple rhyming text. As the children in the book share their preferences, it becomes obvious that such differences in taste are the building blocks of good relationships. At the end the children join hands and chant, "What we all like is . . . making a friend."

As children read this book or listen to it read, they verbalize their agreement or disagreement with each child, reflecting upon their own personal preferences. These might be charted. Children could discuss and talk about how their very best friends are alike and different from them in their personal preferences.

Brewster, Patience. (1991). *Rabbit Inn*. Little, Brown. P, I, 32 pages.

All of the animal guests at the Inn help the rabbit owners spruce the place up for some unexpected guests. After a long day of scrubbing and cleaning, on the last page of the book, they find out who the special guests are.

Children who have helped clean house or spruce up the classroom for visitors will relate to the hard work involved. They can talk about how much easier tasks like that are when friends and family cooperate to get it done. When we respect and appreciate others, we want to help them with their work. Children can relate stories about how they have helped others and might divide into groups to accomplish the tasks that need to be done for the classroom or school.

Bulla, Clyde Robert. (1978). *Keep Running, Allen*. Illus. by Satomi Ichikawa. Harper. P, 32 pages.

Allen is the youngest of a group of children who are running in the hills. He can't keep up and they keep encouraging him by shouting, "Keep running, Allen!" When they finally reach the top of the hill, it is Allen who offers something to really appreciate. He lies on his back and notices the clouds. Everyone has a much more enjoyable adventure when they relax on the grass together.

This is a good example about how younger or smaller people have something positive to offer a group situation. If a class is multi-age grouped, or if there are buddy reading or learning programs, children can talk about the contributions of the youngest to the group. They can also talk about the unique contributions of younger brothers and sisters to their families. The book is also a good example of perseverance on the part of a young child, which fits in with Chapter 11 on diligence, perseverance, and patience.

Damrell, Liz. (1991). *With the Wind*. Illus. by Stephen Marchesi. Orchard. P, 32 pages.

A young boy enjoys with exuberance the thrill of riding horseback. It is not until the next to the last page that the illustrations inform us that this child has a disability. He has a brace on his leg and is placed in a wheelchair after his horseback ride.

Books like this emphasize how little difference a handicap makes. Any child who has been on horseback can relate to this child's feelings about the experience. Having a physical handicap does not make people different on the inside where it counts. From reading this book children might discuss how life might be different for children with physical handicaps and how they might work to make life easier for them. Children might also share their personal experiences with friends who are handicapped. If there are handicapped children in your classroom, this book can be part of an ongoing project in assuring their acceptance.

Davey, Thyrza. (1984). *Waiting for May*. Doubleday. I, 32 pages.

Alec Thomson is an eccentric old man who lives with his dog, Ben, in an old, beached houseboat. Its condition is so bad that the welfare department deems it unfit for habitation. Alec and Ben survive due to the loving care of a family that runs a general store nearby. When the welfare lady threatens to place Alec in a nursing home, he is determined to stay in his houseboat. A devastating storm makes that impossible. Eventually, the neighboring family decides to let Alec stay in their extra room. Alec is an eccentric old sailor like Captain Snap in Roni Schotter's *Captain Snap and the Children of Vinegar Lane*. Both books emphasize the problems faced by older people who have led independent nonconformist lifestyles.

This book should raise the desires of elementary school children to do something to help the aged. For example, it may be possible for the class to establish a relationship with a nearby nursing home. The story also might generate discussion and writing about people who are different—memorable people in the children's lives.

Hahn, Mary Downing. (1983). *Daphne's Book*. Houghton Mifflin. I, 192 pages.

A seventh grade English teacher pairs a bright middle class child with a poor abused child to write a story together. They both learn to use each other's talents and become close friends. The middle class child comes to understand the reality of child abuse and neglect. The poor child takes total responsibility for a younger sibling. And stereotypes are broken.

Children in school might talk about their own stereotypes and prejudices that have been broken by personal experiences. "I used to think Don was a bully because he was so big," a child stated once, "but now I know he is gentle and kind."

Hedderwick, Mairi. (1986). *Katie Morag and the Two Grandmothers*. Little, Brown. P, 32 pages.

Katie Morag lives on an island in the Hebrides with her mother, who is the postmaster and manager of the general store, and her baby brother. Her "Granny Island" raises sheep at the other end of the island, traveling from place to place on a tractor she fixes herself. "Granny Mainland," frail, petite, and pretty, comes to visit and the contrast between the two is striking. Granny Island makes several disparaging comments about Granny Mainland, until Katie recommends Granny Mainland's curlers and shampoo to remove the grime from the bog from Alcina, one of Granny Island's star sheep. Alcina wins best of show and Granny Island discovers a new appreciation for Granny Mainland. They all have a party to celebrate.

The book provides an excellent example of not prejudging someone and of appreciating differences. Children can talk about times when they thought a child might not be nice, but the child ended up being friendly. Or about how they have learned to appreciate children who are different from themselves. The book can be referred to later if a problem arises in which the class is unaccepting of a "different" child.

Heide, Florence Parry & Gilliland, Judith Heide. (1990). *The Day of Ahmed's Secret*. Illus. by Ted Lewin. Lothrop, Lee & Shepard. P, I, 32 pages.

Ahmed, a young boy, delivers fuel in bottles all day as he anticipates telling his secret to his family that night. His secret is that he has learned how to write his name. Ahmed is an Arab, living in Cairo, a city with a culture that shines through brilliantly in both the illustrations and the text of this book. American children will listen in wonder to the adventures of this young lad who, instead of attending school, drives his own donkey cart through the busy streets of Cairo each day.

Children will immediately draw comparisons between Ahmed's life and their own. The contrasts are remarkable. Ahmed works all day long to support his family. American children of the same age attend school and play. Ahmed is alone in a big city and can earn a living for himself, yet he has just learned how to write his name. American children also recall with wonder the time when they learned how to write their names. Extensions could include recalling when they accomplished something like riding their bikes. In spite of all their differences, the feelings underlying such accomplishments are the same, no matter what culture children have as their own. It is not only appreciating and respecting differences, but also recognizing underlying similarities that links people with each other.

Herman, Charlotte. (1991). *Max Malone Makes a Million*. Illus. by Cat Bowman Smith. Henry Holt. P, I, 64 pages.

After Max reads about a get-rich-quick scheme, he sets out on one of his own. When his six-year-old neighbor volunteers to help him, Max just laughs. But in the end, the six-year-old is successful and Max is not.

How often older children don't respect and appreciate the abilities of younger ones. Children will be able to take both sides of this relationship issue— the older child who has scoffed at the abilities of the younger one, and the younger one who has wanted to contribute to a project with an older one, but been shunned. The underlying message that we can respect people of differing ages might lead to children listing the times they have admired individuals who are younger than they are.

Hoffman, Mary. (1991). *Amazing Grace*. Illus. by Caroline Binch. Dial. P, 32 pages.

It is surprising how few contemporary books deal directly with issues of prejudice. Grace desperately wants the role of Peter Pan in a school play, and is an incredibly talented dancer deserving of the part. But because she is a Black and a girl, her classmates determine it is inappropriate for her to play that role. Fortunately, Grace has a very supportive grandmother who helps her deal with her disappointment in a most amazing way.

Children will relate to times when their friends or rules have been unfair to them. They can discuss the issue of prejudice and relate any examples they have seen or experienced in their lives.

Isadora, Rachel. (1991). *At the Crossroads*. Greenwillow. P, I, 32 pages.

Children from a segregated South African township gather at the crossroads to await their fathers' return from 10 months in the mines. The children create homemade musical instruments for the celebration. This is a realistic book about an African experience that has universal underlying emotions—the jubilation at the return of a loved one.

Children can relate to this book by remembering their separation experiences. Some examples might include awaiting the return of a mother from the hospital when a new baby sibling was born, awaiting a parent returning from war, or awaiting a parent or friend's return from traveling. Older children will be fascinated by the segregation issue and about the circumstances under which these men must work, separated from their families for 10 months at a time. Children can chart the occupations of their parents and talk about the pros and cons of different careers, noting differences among the careers represented by their parents and those in books they have read.

Johnston, Tony. (1986). *Pages of Music*. Illus. by Tomie dePaola. Putnam. P, I, 32 pages.

An artist and her son visit the island of Sardinia, where she paints the beautiful landscapes. The poor shepherds share their fogli di musica (a special kind of bread) with them. Years later, the grown boy, now a composer and conductor, never forgets the lovely sounds of the shepherds' pipes and composes an orchestral piece especially for the shepherds of Sardinia. He brings his entire orchestra to the island on Christmas day to share his music with the shepherds.

This story can help children understand that their talents are gifts they can share with the world. You might have a concert in your classroom with those children who would like to share their talents with the others. They might also perform for younger children. Activities like this help children learn to love and appreciate everyone's talents, even when they are different from their own.

Joseph, Lynn. (1990). *Coconut Kind of Day*. Lothrop, Lee & Shepard. P, 32 pages.

A collection of island poems about a day in the life of a Caribbean child. Told in dialect, and rich with tropical images, these poems make obvious the differences in the life of a child on an island and a child in the United States.

Children can recall any experiences visiting or living on an island or any Caribbean experiences which provide a link between this child's experiences and their own. It is by discovering links between ourselves and people of another culture that we discover the basic values which we can appreciate in everyone. A logical followup would be for children to write in poetic form about their days wherever they live and then to compare what they have written to this child's day.

Kline, Suzy. (1991). *Mary Marony and the Snake.* Illus. by Blanche Sims. Putnam. P, I, 64 pages.

Mary Marony stutters and her second grade classmates tease her, especially Marvin Higgins. Mary earns the respect of her fellow students when Marvin's father brings a snake to school and Mary rescues it when it gets loose. Marvin is terrified of snakes.

Children might talk about animals that frighten them and how to overcome those fears. They can write or talk about how it feels to be different. Since all children have at one time or another been teased, they can recall such experiences and discuss how they felt. Perhaps their own feelings will help the children want to avoid such feelings occurring in others and make them think twice before teasing someone else who is different.

Luttrell, Ida. (1990). *Three Good Blankets.* Illus. by Michael McDermott. Atheneum. P, I, 32 pages.

An old woman's daughter buys a new wool blanket for her mother, who lives alone in an old, cold house on a hill. The mother chooses to give the new blanket to her faithful donkey who carries her wood. When her son gives her another new blanket, she gives that one to her goat who provides her with rich, creamy milk. And when her other son gives her a third blanket, she places it over her trusty dog who gives her protection. She keeps a holey blanket for her own use. This story is not only an example of caring for others (in this case the woman for her animals and her children for her) but also of responsible behavior (see Chapter 5 on responsibility), for the woman declines an invitation to come and live with her daughter because her animals depend upon her. The knowledge that her animals are all taken care of warms her through the cold weather of winter.

Children's responses might involve how their pets depend upon them and how they care for their animals. The book can be used in conjunction with discussion and instructions concerning the care of classroom pets, or with other books that focus upon older people who are independent and different from the norm. The children, although disappointed that she does not use the gifts they gave her in the ways that they intended, respect her decision to do with them what she deems most important. Children can discuss the idea that part of respecting others is allowing them to do things differently than we would.

Lyon, George Ella. (1991). *Cecil's Story.* Illus. by Peter Catalanotto. Orchard. P, I, 32 pages.

Using direct questions, Lyon asks readers how they would feel if their father left for the Civil War and returned with a missing arm. That is exactly what happens to the child in the story, but the moral is stated that, even with an arm missing, he is still your papa. You would rejoice at his return.

The fact that physically handicapped people have the same emotions and concerns as nonhandicapped people is a lesson that children need to learn early in their experience. Physical appearance has nothing to do with close human relationships. If there are no physically handicapped children in the classroom, the class might discuss their feelings and fears about having relationships with handicapped children. The class might develop a friendship with some handicapped children and make arrangements to do things together and get to know each other.

Morris, Ann. (1990). *On the Go.* Lothrop, Lee & Shepard. P, I, 32 pages.

This nonfiction book shows in photographs how people move from one place to another in various parts of the world. Each photo is labeled so that you know where it was taken. Children learn how normal it is for people in some parts of the world to carry things on their heads or to use various animals as pack animals. This beautiful book is not only informative, it evokes feelings as well through the illustrations.

Children might graph the different modes of transportation they use to get to school or travel to their grandparents' houses. They might graph the different types of motor vehicles used by their families. Even within a classroom, we are all different. Graphing those differences helps children see themselves as unique individuals.

Ringgold, Faith. (1991). *Tar Beach.* Crown. P, 32 pages.

The "tar beach" is the tarred roof of a Harlem tenement on which residents place blankets to sunbathe. It is a special place where Cassie retreats to dream about life. This story was originally written by Faith Ringgold to accompany her story quilt, and a bit of the quilt is seen on each page until at the end you view the completed work.

Children who don't live in major cities may be quite surprised to find that the roofs of apartment buildings create similar moods as the beaches some of them may visit in the summer. All children have special places they like to visit where they can contemplate life's challenges. Children might write about their "special places." The class could create their own tar beach quilt of pictures of the children's very special places—all of which would be different.

Schotter, Roni. (1990). *Captain Snap and the Children of Vinegar Lane.* Illus. by Marcia Sewall. Orchard Books. P, 32 pages.

Everybody is afraid of Captain Snap, an eccentric old sailor who lives at the end of Vinegar Lane. But the children are curious and visit him periodically. On one visit they find that he is ill, so they gather a blanket and food for the old man. When he recovers, he turns his junky house into a craft museum of homemade art, perhaps in gratitude to the community that cared for him while he was ill.

Caring for a person in need, especially an older person not in the family, is a moral of importance in this story. Children also learn that you cannot judge a book by its cover, for the ill-tempered old man is actually a very creative artist. How important it is not to jump to conclusions about people before you know them. The children were actually afraid of this old man early in the story. This book might lead children into action to help people in need, such as the homeless in their community. It also creates the climate for using junk, normally considered valueless, to make creative works. Following the model used by Captain Snap, children might turn part of their classroom into a museum to display the items they have created. Inviting others to see displays provides a genuine audience for project work.

Shelby, Anne. (1991). *Potluck.* Illus. by Irene Trivas. Orchard. P, 32 pages.

Potluck is an alphabet book. For each letter of the alphabet, a child whose name begins with that letter uses an action that begins with that letter to bring a food that begins with that letter to a potluck meal. The illustrations, lavishly exuberant and colorful, depict children of all racial and cultural backgrounds and foods from around the world. But the nice part about the book is that it reflects American life where everyone, no matter what their origin, enjoys ethnic foods. This counter-stereotype is typified by Ben, an African-American, who brought bagels to the feast.

Children often reject foods that are different from what they are used to eating, especially if they have been raised on a limited diet. Yet gradually foods such as spaghetti, pizza, and tacos have become staples of the American diet. Discussion and charting of children's favorite foods could lead to a potluck meal in the classroom, where children each bring to school a recipe reflecting their ethnic origins, and the class prepares a potluck meal. Food can be an excellent entree to appreciating different cultures.

Spinelli, Jerry. (1990). *Maniac Magee.* Little, Brown. I, 154 pages.

This winner of the Newbery Award involves a high school dropout who teaches an illiterate former minor league baseball player how to read when the old man helps provide the homeless boy with shelter. This is a touching story of human relationships, people needing one another, and people caring for one another. At one point in the story, Maniac, a White boy, is taken in by a Black family that lives on the predominantly Black side of town.

Older elementary and middle school children might discuss issues of stereotyping and prejudiced thinking. They might write about people much older or younger than they are, or people of a different race, with whom they have had special relationships. If they have had contacts with homeless people, a discussion of this national problem would be beneficial.

Stevenson, James. (1991). *The Worst Person's Christmas.* Greenwillow. P, I, 32 pages.

In cartoon format, a Scrooge-like worst person refuses to celebrate Christmas until some neighborhood children give him a present, and through a series of comical coincidences, he is forced to be jovial for the holidays.

Children can talk about people they know who seem grouchy and the ethics of being nice to someone who isn't nice in return. They can learn through discussions how their actions and demeanor affect other people.

Turkle, Brinton. (1982). *Thy Friend, Obadiah.* Penguin. P, 32 pages.

Obadiah's sisters and brothers tease him because a seagull has befriended him and follows him everywhere. At first Obadiah submits to their taunting and tries to throw a stone at the bird to discourage it, but that doesn't work. When the bird disappears for several days, Obadiah has an opportunity to really think about his values. He misses the bird and is concerned about it. When he finds it on the fishing wharf with its beak caught in a fish hook, the bird lets him come close and remove the fish hook. Obadiah has helped his very special friend, and in fact probably saved its life.

Children can talk about and write about how they have helped animals that have appeared to be helpless. They can also brainstorm ideas on how to respond when someone is teasing them, and compare Obadiah's reaction to that of the cow and the pig in Bernard Most's *The Cow that Went OINK.*

Vagin, Vladimir & Asch, Frank. (1989). *Here Comes the Cat!* Scholastic. P, 32 pages.

This is the first book ever written and illustrated by a Russian and American together. In their introduction, the authors explain that they felt as if they were living next door to each other during the creation of the book, although they really lived a continent apart. The story is about some fearful mice who are afraid of a cat. But when the cat finally appears, it is pulling a cart containing a huge cheese, a great feast for the mice.

After discussing the historical and political importance of these two writer-illustrators working together, children might choose people they would not normally work with, people with whom they are not close friends, to complete a project. They might try to analyze their own talents and team up with a child whose talents are complementary.

Williams, Karen Lynn. (1991). *When Africa Was Home.* Orchard. P, I, 32 pages.

Peter, a White child, has been raised by an African nanny while his parents were working for the Peace Corps in Malawi. Peter has absolutely no desire to return to the United States where children have to wear shoes and eat using utensils. He sadly says goodbye to all of his African extended family and friends. In the U.S. he hates the cold snow and dreams of his former home in Africa. At the end of the story, the family returns to Africa and Peter is very happy to be home again. This partially autobiographical account shares a different perspective on American life and gives children an example of how other people see our culture.

Children almost always prefer the culture in which they were raised, and sometimes look down upon other cultures that are different. After reading Peter's perspectives on American life, children might imagine what it would be like to live in a place where you could go without shoes all the time, eat with your fingers, walk for transportation, and in other ways live differently from the way they are used to living.

SUMMARY

The first step in helping children become empathic toward others is alerting them to the uniqueness of every individual so that they can learn to appreciate traits and qualities that are different from their own. Sharing any children's book that reflects a different culture from that of the reader or listener is a beginning step to helping children respect and appreciate others. Because children relate to the story characters in books like *The Day of Ahmed's Secret, Tar Beach, A Coconut Kind of Day, At the Crossroads,* and *Thy Friend, Obadiah,* they learn to appreciate children from other cultures whose lives may differ greatly from their own, but who at the same time have some of the same attitudes and feelings about what is important in life. Several other books go beyond just sharing a story from another culture to directly confronting cultural or racial or personal difference issues. *When Africa Was Home, Here Comes the Cat, Maniac Magee,* and *Amazing Grace* are some examples.

Another way prejudices arise and people are stereotyped is by age. In *Max Malone Makes a Million,* Max discovers that a younger friend is better able to make money than he is. Children need to learn to respect people of all different ages, which for older children can require a degree of humility.

When we respect and appreciate others, we are more likely to be thoughtful and considerate of others. Kind and thoughtful behavior creates a caring classroom, a place where children are free to take risks in what they say and do with each other, a haven for thoughtful discussion and writing. The guests in *Rabbit Inn* thoughtfully help clean the Inn when some unexpected guests are due to arrive. The theme of several books is reaching out to those who are different in some way. Children display caring behavior to eccentric senior citizens in *Captain Snap and the Children of Vinegar Lane, Maniac Magee, Waiting for May, The Worst Person's Christmas,* and *Better with Two.* The mental health of our nation depends upon individuals who love and appreciate others enough to become involved in the care of those who are less fortunate.

People who are different because of disabilities are featured in three of the books: *Cecil's Story, Mary Marony and the Snake,* and *With the Wind.* Understanding, accepting, and helping people with disabilities in ways that are not condescending are the goals of sharing this kind of book with children.

A nation such as ours, populated with people from so many ethnic backgrounds, will only become a safe and happy place when people value differences, rather than condone uniformity. Several books celebrate the differences among people. *On the Go, Potluck, Pages of Music,* and *Katie Morag and the Two Grandmothers* are examples. Unfortunately, much of what is presented in the media promotes the kind of unthinking conformity which builds peer pressure for children. Helping children become independent thinkers and actors, therefore, is a critical part of the moral education curriculum.

CHAPTER 10

Ecological Values

RATIONALE

The acquisition of ecological awareness and development of responsible environmental behavior are major educational issues for the 1990s. Since our goal is not just to help children become more knowledgeable but also to promote their active involvement in working toward a more livable future, our teaching needs to focus upon attitudes and behaviors as well as on knowledge.

Research has shown differences in children's attitudes based on their age and their own environmental experiences. Younger children are often more fearful of the natural environment and more negative toward wildlife, particularly animals, than are older children. Further, children who live in urban areas and visit places such as zoos and parks have less positive attitudes toward the environment than rural children. Today, as the number of children growing up in urban settings increases, opportunities for direct involvement with the natural environment diminish. Many children receive their first introduction to the natural environment through reading and watching television. Using good environmental literature in our classrooms thus becomes of paramount importance. Books can provide the link between the child's world and the outside world; they can become a springboard to discussion about facts, attitudes, and behaviors toward the environment and a catalyst for environmental action in classrooms and homes.

When selecting literature with environmental content, it is helpful to note that nonfiction books present more facts and discuss behaviors more than fiction books, but fiction books raise more issues and deal more with attitudes. A comprehensive approach which includes both fiction and nonfiction is likely, then, to have the most impact upon children. Since 70 percent of all children's titles published each year are fiction, it may take a concerted effort to create a balance by including nonfiction in this aspect of the moral education curriculum.

A second consideration in book selection is the type of illustration in the book. Children associate photographs and realistic illustrations with factual information and cartoons and expressionistic illustrations with fantasy. They prefer realistic illustrations. Related to this issue is the number of books which are somewhat accurate in content, except for anthropomorphic animals that wear human clothing or speak to each other and humans. While these books can present some accurate information, attitudes, and even behaviors, it is important that children understand that animals really don't talk, think, or behave like humans. Children are less likely to believe what they read when it is presented in this "animals as people" format, so the adult might have to clarify or provide experiences which make the content more believable.

A third consideration when selecting books for young children is that the books that are most effective are those which children can relate to their own lives. For this reason, backyard stories about insects and trees are more potent than books about rainforests and deserts, habitats most children have not directly experienced. It is easy to get mesmerized by the gorgeous illustrations of exotic places and forget that the most important environmental decisions are made by people in their own environs.

Environmental issues command much attention in recently published children's books, particularly books with science content. If books containing just knowledge are shared as a part of the curriculum, it is up to the teacher, librarian, or parent to carry them a step farther and use strategies that promote responses that include attitudes and behaviors. Other issues critical in selecting picture books with environmental content are the type and quality of illustrations, the degree of anthropomorphism present in the text, the immediacy of the environment to the life of the child, and the balance between fiction and nonfiction literature.

CLASSROOM VIGNETTE

It is not often that children will be moved by reading a book and participating in classroom activities to carry on with the idea at home, but that is exactly what happened when Kathy shared the book, *Miss Rumphius*, by Barbara Cooney (Viking, 1982) with a class of second graders.

Miss Rumphius is a fictional biography, in picture book format, of Alice Rumphius. As a child, she tells her grandfather that one day when she is grown up she will go to faraway places and live by the sea, as he does. Her grandfather approves, but explains that there is a third thing she must also do, and that is to make the world more beautiful. Alice promises that she will and, years later, becomes known as the Lupine Lady who scatters lupine seeds all over the coast of Maine.

Not only is this the story of an independent lady who takes charge of her life, it is also the story of a person who cares for the beauty of the landscape. Kathy titled a piece of chart paper, "How I Can Make the World More Beautiful," and was surprised at the many and varied responses from some second graders. "Clean the room up," "Pick up trash," "Don't litter," "Recycle," and "Plant flowers" were a few of the responses. This chart served as a discussion tool for her classes as children shared with others what they knew about recycling and ways to keep their house, school, and community looking beautiful.

As a culminating activity, each child was given a mixture of wild-flower seeds. The information about how to plant them, how long they would take to grow, and how often to water them, were read. The children then chose a place near their classroom to plant the seeds. Soon, signs and labels, in invented spelling, were seen telling others not to step in this very special area. In order to develop responsibility, the children created a watering chart with two students assigned each day to fill the watering can and dampen the flower garden.

"I'm going home and tell my mom that we need to plant flowers around our house," said Sarah, excited as they worked on their project. If we can nurture in our young children an appreciation for the beauty of our land, there is hope that the world will be in capable hands in years to come.

BOOK REVIEWS AND CURRICULAR EXTENSIONS

In the following bibliography, the grade-level designation "P" means the book might be more valuable for the primary grades, kindergarten to grade 3. The designation "I" means the intermediate grades 3-5.

Adoff, Arnold. (1991). *In for Winter, Out for Spring.* Illus. by Jerry Pinkney. Harcourt Brace Jovanovich. P, 32 pages.

This beautiful book contains poems about a family's experiences in each of the seasons. In addition to traditional seasonal activities, this family cares for an injured bird and adopts a stray dog, two common behaviors of families that care about animals.

This book could inspire children to write their own poems about their favorite aspects of each season and their favorite memories of family experiences. Stories about trying to save birds or adopting pets may well be a natural outflow from this book.

Albert, Burton. (1991). *Where Does the Trail Lead?* Illus. by Brian Pinkney. Simon & Schuster. P, 32 pages.

A boy follows a trail on an island, noticing wildflowers, old railroad tracks, tide-pools of periwinkles, wild animals, blueberries, sand dunes, deserted shanties, and an old beached rowboat. The smell of the sea is always with him as he reaches his family gathered around a campfire at the sea's edge.

Many children can recall hiking on a trail or even exploring a small path near their homes. So much of what lives near a trail goes unnoticed until children are helped to see and appreciate the natural beauty right at hand. An obvious follow-up activity from reading this book would be to visit a nature center and take a hike on some of the trails. Children can compare their observations to those of the book's protagonist.

Aronsky, Jim. (1990). *Near the Sea.* Lothrop. P, I, 32 pages.

Near the Sea is a portfolio of paintings that document Aronsky's experiences on a small Maine island. He paints bluefish, the channel, gulls and dry rocks, an outland tidal pool, a marsh, a cave, and a boat yard. This personal narrative can inspire similar activities in class.

Children can be led to observe more closely the habitats near their homes and the ones they visit. These can be painted and written about. When they love and appreciate their own personal environments, children are more likely to take actions to preserve them.

Baines, Chris. (1989). *The Old Boot.* Crocodile Books. P, I, 32 pages.

Baines explains how common animals utilize environments close at hand. She describes in detail the story of how creatures of nature use an old discarded boot. This story makes the lives of insects particularly interesting and demonstrates the development of a miniature ecosystem.

Children can replicate Baines' book. All it takes is an old boot and some willing insects. The children's observations can lead to a book of their own.

Baines, Chris. (1989). *The Picnic.* Crocodile Books. P, 32 pages.

In a similar fashion, Baines tells how the different animals in nature utilize the remnants of a picnic left by a group of children. It features many familiar insects and other animals. Try taking the children on a picnic, reading the book before, during, and after the experience.

Bash, Barbara. (1989). *Desert Giant: The World of the Saguaro Cactus.* Little, Brown. P, I, 32 pages.

This book shares the beauty and character of desert life. It helps counteract the stereotypical thinking that allows people to dump things in the desert because "nothing" lives there. It is a nonfiction book presenting information but, discussion and extensions such as similar observations in the children's own environment, will help develop an awareness that life is everywhere and that every habitat needs protection.

Bash, Barbara. (1990). *Urban Roosts: Where Birds Nest in the City.* Little, Brown. P, I, 32 pages.

The exciting part about this book is that it takes place in a city. Urban children and visitors can appreciate all the wildlife that exists even in an urban setting. The close-up sketches and beautiful full-color illustrations show vividly how birds have adapted to city living. Urban children can be led to discover the urban roosts near their schools and homes. Visitors from local nature clubs can help the children learn what they can do to support wildlife in an urban environment.

Burningham, John. (1989). *Hey! Get Off Our Train.* Crown. P, 32 pages.

A young boy has a dream that he rescues five endangered animals when his toy train becomes real. When asked to get off the train, each animal has a plea. The elephant begs, "Please take me with you on your train. Someone is coming to cut off my tusks, and soon there will be none of us left." The seal is escaping polluted water which has been overfished; the crane is finding wetlands that have been drained; the tiger is seeking forests; and the polar bear is running from those who would use his fur for a coat.

Although this book combines fantasy with reality and deals with exotic animals not within most children's environment, it still offers an opportunity for children to learn factual information about extinction. Since the boy takes action and rescues these animals, a follow-up discussion might influence groups of children to join the ecology movement in an active way. Such in-school discussions have actually proven fruitful: a second grade purchased over 5,000 acres of rain forest. Another class adopted a manatee.

Cole, Sheila. (1991). *When the Rain Stops.* Illus. by Henri Sorensen. Lothrop, Lee & Shepard. P, 32 pages.

Lella and her father find their blackberry picking interrupted by a rainstorm. After the storm they notice all the differences in the habitat caused by the rainstorm.

Children can recall being outside in the rain. They can talk about the effects of rain on their lives and their neighborhoods. They might also go berry picking as a class, which might cause them to be more sensitive to and appreciative of these habitats. Their writings based upon this experience might range from narrative stories about berry picking, including the feelings experienced on the outing, to expository writings explaining how to be an efficient berry picker or on the different kinds of berries that are available and their possible uses. These writings might be shared with the community as a way to encourage others to venture outdoors and appreciate their environment.

Cowcher, Helen. (1990). *Antarctica.* Farrar, Straus, Giroux. P, I, 32 pages.

This beautifully illustrated picture book shares information about the Adeile and Emperor Penguins on Antarctica, including the fact that helicopters and ships greatly disturb the natural living conditions of these animals who must fight harsh conditions for survival.

One first grade class was so moved by reading this book that they wrote away to a number of places to find out more about this issue and others like it. They ended up adopting a manatee (since they lived in Florida).

Cowcher, Helen. (1991). *Tigress.* Farrar, Straus, Giroux. P, I, 32 pages.

A tigress walks out of a sanctuary in Africa to find food for her two cubs. After she kills a sheep and a camel, the local herders decide that something must be done, as they cannot afford such losses. They contemplate poisoning the tigress, but after sitting down with the ranger, decide to frighten it back to the sanctuary with firecrackers.

This book provides a wonderful example of solving an environmental problem peacefully. It presents both sides of the issue: the environmentalists who want to save tigers from extinction and the local herders who need to make a living. Both sides win through their ability to compromise.

Dewey, Jennifer Owings. (1991). *A Night and Day in the Desert.* Little, Brown. P, 32 pages.

Beautifully colored and realistic drawings and a clear, simple text combine to reveal the excitement of animal activity during a night and a day in the desert. Since many people think of the desert as a barren habitat, this book is informative. It includes the activity of all kinds of wildlife—reptiles and insects as well as mammals. This nonfiction book describes how each animal survives in its desert home environment. The fact that the author lives in New Mexico lends authenticity to the book.

Prior to sharing this book, children can write down their impressions of a desert, listing what they know about its plants and animals. Then, after sharing the book, have the children discuss how active and alive a desert really is and, perhaps, how much more it contains than they had realized. After reading this book, children might extend their knowledge of desert habitats by looking for more information about the animals written about in this book.

Dobson, C. (1989). *Fred's TV.* Firefly Books. P, 32 pages.

Fred can't control his TV viewing habits so his parents remove the set to the backyard. Soon birds are nesting in it and Fred becomes engrossed in viewing them. He learns that every living thing needs a home with specific characteristics.

Other children can learn this too, by recording their observations of animal homes. They should make a list of the attributes of each home and deduce, with teacher help, the reasons behind each attribute.

Fife, Dale H. *The Empty Lot.* Illus. by Jim Aronsky. Little, Brown. P, I, 32 pages.

Harry Hale decides to sell a lot that he owns out in the country, but before he sells it, he decides to pay it a visit. While there he learns about how rich his lot is as a habitat for wildlife, and decides not to sell the lot after all.

Most children live near a vacant lot or green space and can visit it and explore all the species of life that are supported by that special place. After children have conducted actual observational research in the habitats near their homes, they might produce reports of that information and disseminate their findings through local environmental action groups or their local newspaper.

George, William T. (1991). *Fishing at Long Pond.* Illus. by Lindsay Barrett George. Greenwillow. P, I, 24 pages.

In this simple book, Katie and her grandfather go fishing on a pond. While they fish, they develop a sense of wonder at the bird, animal, and plant life that they observe.

Many children go fishing and use that time to make observations about the environment. These children will want to talk and write about their observations. There may be some children in the class who are opposed to fishing, as they are to hunting, which can provide varying viewpoints from which to discuss the moral ethic of killing for food.

Gibbons, Gail. (1989). *Monarch Butterfly*. Holiday House. P, 32 pages.

Monarch Butterfly follows the life cycle of that insect and includes instructions on how to raise a monarch, an activity that could be carried out in the classroom.

The book shares the ways people celebrate the migration of the monarch butterfly. Children might have their own celebrations for butterflies and see how many kinds they can identify.

Ichikawa, Saromi. (1991). *Nora's Duck*. Philomel. P, 32 pages.

Nora brings a sick duck to her family doctor in a heartwarming story that animal lovers will enjoy.

Many children have tried to save a bird that has flown into a window or a wild animal that has been injured. Caring for wildlife can help children learn how to better care for the world. As children learn about the food chain through reading this book, they will see that even such practices as spraying for insects have an impact on the wildlife they see daily. Children would enjoy talking with people in the community who are known for caring for wildlife.

Jeffers, Susan. (1991). *Brother Eagle, Sister Sky: A Message from Chief Seattle*. Dial. P, I, 32 pages.

Accompanied by 28 full-color paintings, the text recreates the words attributed to a great American Indian chief, Chief Seattle, over 100 years ago. The message is simple: this earth and every living creature on it is sacred. It is a call to people everywhere to care for and preserve the environment.

The words of Chief Seattle inspired Susan Jeffers' paintings and might inspire school children to paint environmental scenes and creatures as well. The class could have a gallery of paintings dedicated to the preservation of the environment.

Lehrman, F. (1990). *Loving the Earth: A Sacred Landscape Book for Children*. Celestial Arts. I, 48 pages.

Loving the Earth teaches children respect for the earth by introducing environmental concepts with simple things for children to do. For example, it introduces air pollution by asking the children to take a deep breath indoors and outdoors. The book helps children understand what they can do in their own lives to impact on large global environmental problems.

Lobel, Anita. (1990). *Alison's Zinnia*. Greenwillow. P, I, 32 pages.

Each girl, named in alphabetical order in this alphabet book, does something to care for a flower for the next child in the book. The ethic of being thoughtful of one another is blended with the wild flower theme.

Integrated into a study of wild flowers, the gorgeous paintings in *Alison's Zinnia* inspire children to notice and learn about wild flowers in their environs. Such a study might also encourage them to replant wildflowers on the school grounds or other deserving sites. This book would be a good one to share along with Barbara Cooney's *Miss Rumphius*.

McDonald, Megan. (1990). *Is This a House for Hermit Crab?* Illus. by S. D. Schindler. A Orchard. P, 32 pages.

This simple story with repetitive language is about a hermit crab who, having outgrown his own house, goes looking for a new one. Several of the homes the crab tries are man-made—a fishing net, a pail, and an old tin can. These can promote a discussion of the impact of humans on the life of crustaceans. This may even lead to some action on recycling or litter control. This book won the IRA Children's Book Award for 1990.

Melville, Herman. (1991). *Catskill Eagle.* Illus. by Thomas Locker. Philomel. I, 32 pages.

Thomas Locker has painted very inspiring illustrations to accompany Herman Melville's words about the majestic mountain eagle. This very intimate view of an endangered animal cannot help but encourage children to become activists.

Children might investigate endangered species near where they live and learn how they can work to protect those animals. They might collect beautiful artwork or photography of endangered species for a classroom bulletin. The artists in the class might be inspired by the work of Thomas Locker to produce paintings of local endangered species.

Mendoza, George. (1990). *Were You a Wild Duck, Where Would You Go?* Illus. by and Osborn-Smith. Steward, Tabor & Chang. P, I, 32 pages.

Were You a Wild Duck, Where Would You Go? presents information about what has happened to bird nesting places and calls out to the reader, "Let us save the marshes and the trees. Let us protect the prairies and love the land." No specific strategies are suggested for doing these things. In the book birds speak directly to the reader: "Mallard is my name. I am a wetland bird." The reader is also drawn into the book through questions which require thoughtful reflection, such as, "What would you do if you found your land scorched, the land where you nest is stretched barren without trees, your glacial paradise gone?" Man's greed is listed as the source of the problems.

Children can role-play local birds making similar observations in their own neighborhood. They can research what is being done in their area which is helpful or might impact harmfully upon the bird population. They might join efforts to stop the depletion of nesting sites for various birds.

Orr, Katherine. (1990). *My Grandpa and the Sea.* Carolrhoda. P, 32 pages.

Some books have very direct and didactic messages to impart about how we should behave. Sometimes that didactic approach hurts the story being told. This is not the case in *My Grandpa and the Sea.* Grandpa is a fisherman on St. Lucia. The Caribbean views in the illustrations are spectacular. The story is fresh and forthright until the end where Grandpa is quoted as saying, "If we give something for everything we take we will always meet with abundance."

A very direct moral to the story, but one that fits so perfectly, it is not offensive. Children might list ways they can give something back to the earth in their daily lives, then follow up with one or two projects to be done at school. This book reflects the ethic of responsibility for the earth in a similar manner to Barbara Cooney's *Miss Rumphius.*

Paladino, Catherine. (1991). *Our Vanishing Farm Animals: Saving America's Rare Breeds.* Joy Street Books/Little, Brown. P, I, 32 pages.

In this photo essay we learn how eight animals, whose genetic traits may well hold answers to the future of farming, must be protected. Paladino shares the roles these gentle, hardy, and often multipurpose animals play on the family farm and shows how a few American children and adults are fighting against their possible extinction.

Urban children know little about the importance of animals to farm cultures. This book shares in a vivid way the importance of these animals and gives all children strategies for becoming active in the movement to restore our endangered environment. The highest possible response to this type of literature is supporting children's active participation in movements such as the one described in this book.

Parsons, Alexandra. (1990). *Amazing Spiders.* Knopf. P, I, 32 pages.

Amazing Spiders helps children understand and appreciate the spider's role in the environment. Striking full-color photographs and fascinating information make this book especially good for oral reading to a group. Spiders are very accessible for study by children. While this book doesn't directly contain any moral values, it does share the value of spiders and makes it less likely that children would be destructive of them. Used in conjunction with a science study project, an attractive book such as this can foster appreciation of creatures with an historically scary reputation.

Peet, Bill. (1966). *Farewell to Shady Glade.* Houghton Mifflin. P, I, 46 pages.

The animals are terrified when the bulldozers come to demolish their homes in Shady Glade in order to build a shopping center. The animals join together and move further into the country to establish a new home.

This book leaves the impression that there is always another place in the country to move when building takes place, but it also points out that progress may have its negative side effects. Linked to *Little House* by Virginia Lee Burton (1978, Houghton Mifflin), the topic of historical preservation vs. demolition might provide an excellent springboard for a study of the children's home towns and how these issues are decided locally.

Peet, Bill. (1975). *The Gnats of Knotty Pine.* Houghton Mifflin. P, I, 46 pages.

The animals are all bemoaning the start of hunting season. They hold a group meeting to plan ways to foil the hunters. The gnats, the smallest animals of all, create a plan to bombard the hunters as they enter the woods, causing them to retreat before they can even begin their hunt.

This strong antihunting message will generate some discussion in a classroom of children who have differing views on the topic. Since the gnats take action, children might be encouraged to explore ways they too, even though small, can take action in support of the causes they believe in.

Ryder, Joanne. (1991). *When the Woods Hum.* Morrow. P, 32 pages.

This book shares a family's love of nature and celebrates the arrival every 17 years of the cicadas. When they emerge, after their long period of growth, the cicadas do no damage to the environment, but provide a lovely song for all to enjoy.

Insects like cicadas make night noises in many places. Children who learn to appreciate insects in their own backyards are more likely to care for their environment than children who only read about exotic animals. After reading this book, children might want to study the insects in the school yard or at home.

Simon, Seymour. (1990). *Deserts.* Morrow. P, I, 32 pages.

In *Deserts*, Seymour Simon mentions that people have differing attitudes toward deserts. To some, deserts are barren wastelands, but to others, deserts are alive with mystery and wonder. Simon's gorgeous photographs make deserts come alive and provide detailed information about differences among some of the world's most famous deserts. Maps depict the most famous deserts while their plants and animals are described in words and pictures.

Many commonly held beliefs about deserts (such as that they must be hot and sandy) are corrected. Although mainly meant to inform, this book presents attitudes as well. A theme study on deserts might result in many reports researched by children about the plant and animal life native to that habitat. An appropriate book link might be made with Barbara Bash's *Desert Giant: The World of the Saguaro Cactus*. If an environment that is perceived to be as barren as a desert is full of life, children can imagine how rich their habitats are, which could lead to more caring behavior.

Slote, Elizabeth. (1991). *Nelly's Garden*. Tambourine. P, I, 32 pages.

During all seasons of the year Nelly Dragon visits her very special garden behind her house. She watches snowflakes in January, collects bugs in July, and jumps in the leaves in November.

This book would be a wonderful springboard to discussion and writing about special places where children play outdoors. In these special places children often notice vegetation and animals that go unnoticed in other settings. When children learn to love and appreciate special outdoor places where they play, they are ready to gradually expand this appreciation to the world beyond their immediate environs.

Twinn, Michael. (1990). *The Tower*. Illus. by Arlette Lavie. Child's Play. P, 32 pages.

A theme of world destruction through the technological "progress" of humanity is found in *The Tower*. A powerful leader comes to the realization that ecological action is necessary for the survival of people on the earth. Though the text is artificially rhymed and the message is didactic (detracting from the quality of the literature), the illustrations and theme make the book a worthwhile one to share with children.

This book might be an appropriate one to memorize and present as a play. It makes a good book link to Bill Peet's *Farewell to Shady Glade*.

Wildsmith, Brian. (1979). *Hunter and His Dog*. Oxford. P, I, 32 pages.

Brian Wildsmith's *Hunter and His Dog* carries a strong antihunting message. The dog, trained by the hunter to bring injured birds to him, instead nurses them to health by bringing them bread. When the hunter discovers the dog's secret, he gives up the sport he has enjoyed for years.

Children can explore the pros and cons of hunting, study regulations regarding hunting, and entertain speakers with opposing views.

THEME STUDY ON TREES

Because trees occur in most environments and are close at hand for environmental study, they make an ideal focus for books containing moral issues related to the environment. And since there are a number of excellent children's books on this topic, a more indepth study in this area seems appropriate. The following books have clear links with each other both in their content and in the environmental messages they contain.

Arnold, Caroline. (1989). *The Terrible Hodag.* Illus. by Lambert Davis. Harcourt Brace Jovanovich. P, 32 pages.

When the boss man makes unreasonable demands upon some lumbermen to clear the hillside and get the lumber to the mill by the end of the week, a terrible Hodag (fictitious monster whom they fear) comes to their rescue. Although this is a story about a mythical talking beast who was featured in stories told in logging camps in the West, the ecological message at the end is clear. The lumberjack vows that, "From now on, we will always be sure to leave part of the forest for the Hodag."

Children can visit local building sites and observe or interview the supervisors to learn about what has been left "for the Hodag."

Ayres, Pam. (1988). *When Dad Cuts Down the Chestnut Tree.* Illus. by Graham Percy. Knopf. P, 32 pages.

Two children decide that the benefits of the chestnut tree in their yard outweigh the disadvantage of having to rake leaves and the many potential uses for the wood. Told in gentle rhyme, with clear illustrations, the book presents many uses for wood, but in the end comes down on the side of valuing the living tree. Children can debate the value of trees both dead and alive. A two-sided chart will help organize and clarify their thinking during the debate.

Bash, Barbara. (1989). *Tree of Life: The World of the African Baobab.* Little, Brown. P, I, 32 pages.

After reading this book, you can't help but fall in love with the baobab tree which grows on the dry savannahs of Africa. Twice a year when the rains come, the tree leafs out and starts to hum with life. Birds like the yellow-collared lovebird, the mosque swallow, and the orange-bellied parrot build nests in the tree. Tiny insects such as sweat bees, cotton stainer bugs, and long-tailed mealybugs make the tree buzz with activity. And at night the white flowers of the tree begin to open while bushbabies and fruit bats feast upon the nectar. During the day a variety of larger mammals feed on the leaves and petals. To the African people, the baobab is more than a source of honey. Its bark is stripped for baskets and rope; its fruit is made into candy and sweet drinks; and its roots and leaves are used as medicine. It is no wonder this is called the tree of life!

While we may not have baobab trees in our yards, we do have other species and when children examine them carefully they will undoubtedly find many kinds of living creatures on them and learn to appreciate living trees more through that experience. One popular activity is to choose a single tree and make weekly journal entries about its seasonal changes and the animal and plant life that inhabits it.

Cherry, Lynn. (1990). *The Great Kapok Tree: A Tale of the Amazon Rainforest.* Harcourt Brace Jovanovich. P, I, 32 pages.

A man discovers a multitude of life in the rainforest which gives him second thoughts about cutting down a kapok tree. A world map identifies the locations of tropical rainforests.

After reading this book children can list ways to avoid using wood and paper and to recycle those materials. They might make labels for the trees in their school yard to inform others about each tree and the species that find life on it. Planting trees in their school yard will provide homes for more insects and birds.

Florian, Douglas. (1990). *Discovering Trees.* Alladin Books. P, 32 pages.

The life cycle of a tree is presented in this nonfiction book, which encourages children to go outside and look at trees. This book would make a nice companion to Natalia Romanova's *Once There Was a Tree* and Chris Van Allsburg's *Just a Dream.*

Romanova, Natalia. (1985). *Once There Was a Tree.* Illus. by Gennady Spirin. Dial. P, 32 pages.

The life cycle of a tree is depicted, including its interactions with humans as a small part of that cycle. Told by a Russian author, and originally published in Russia, this book underlines the international nature of appreciation for living plants. With very little text and striking illustrations, the book's greatest impact is visual. Children will enjoy perusing it independently.

Van Allsburg, Chris. (1990). *Just a Dream.* Houghton Mifflin. P, I, 32 pages.

Just a Dream shows Ben at first inconsiderate of his environment, throwing paper on the sidewalk and not sorting the trash. He is scornful of his neighbor's birthday present, a tree. After some horrible dreams, where he is transported into an environmentally scary future, Ben mends his ways, picks up his trash, sorts the garbage, and asks for a tree for his birthday. His last dream is years later as he rests under two tall trees, planted years ago by two very thoughtful children.

A story like this one might lead children to plant trees, work on recycling projects, and be more careful with their trash.

SUMMARY

As might be expected, there are more nonfiction titles in this chapter than in other chapters in this book. The books tend to be elaborately illustrated, and therefore very appealing visually. Many of the books contain content very appealing to older children, which can also be shared with younger children because of the outstanding illustrations that will captivate them while the book is being read aloud.

Most of the books in this chapter share information about the habitats of plants and animals with the underlying assumption that if people are better informed about habitats, they may take a more active role in preserving them. A number of the books talk about the habitats of specific animals that are not endangered: *Amazing Spiders, Monarch Butterfly,* and *Is This a House for Hermit Crab?* Others talk about habitats that support many plants and animals: *A Night and Day in the Desert, Where Does the Trail Lead?, Near the Sea, Deserts, Urban Roosts,* and *When the Woods Hum.* Several mention a tree or cactus that is an ecological world unto itself: *Tree of Life, The Great Kapok Tree,* and *Desert Giant.*

Since one important determinant of how much children get from their reading is whether they can relate what they read to their own personal experience, it becomes important to share books about common environments that children might encounter every day. *The Old Boot, The Picnic, Fred's TV, The Empty Lot, When the Rain Stops, Fishing at Long Pond,* and *Nellie's Garden* are good backyard ecology choices.

Trees are a popular topic for environmental books. From reading these books, children can learn how valuable trees are, not only as a support to many other plants and animals, but also for their wood products. The mini-theme on trees contains all of the books that center on the tree theme.

Many more books show caring behaviors on the part of people for endangered species or simply for their environment. *Miss Rumphius* and *Alison's Zinnia* show people caring for flowers that make the world a more beautiful place. The deeper issues of the value of flowers to insects are not mentioned in these books. Books about saving animals nearing extinction are numerous. We have included *Our Vanishing Farm Animals, Hey! Get Off Our Train, Catskill Eagle, Antarctica,* and *Were You a Wild Duck, Where Would You Go?*

Several books confront issues head on and openly share attitudes about preservation and conservation. *Tigress* presents both sides of an issue: what to do to preserve animals nearing extinction while at the same time allowing the local population to make a living. *Loving the Earth* presents many strategies for children to become actively involved in working toward improving the environment. *My Grandpa and the Sea* presents a specific case of a family purposely returning something to the earth every time they remove something from it. *Farewell to Shady Glade* and *The Tower* both confront the issue of urban growth as detrimental to wildlife. *Brother Eagle, Sister Sky* shares the Indian perspective that we are not in control of the earth, but brothers and sisters sharing a rich habitat for life. Two books present a strong antihunting ethic: *Hunter and His Dog* and *The Gnats of Knotty Pine.*

Students are likely to take direct personal and group actions to help heal the environment after reading these books. There may be fewer written responses and more discussion and project responses. While all such responses can be appropriate, it is the ones that affect our daily lives that will have the most lasting impact upon the environment.

CHAPTER 11

Diligence, Perseverance, and Patience

RATIONALE

Commercial advertising, lotteries, and other aspects of today's society mesmerize individuals into believing that luck, chance, and free giveaways exist. Yet the old fashioned values involved in the work ethic are what benefit people most in the long run. Children who rely upon luck have an external locus of control. They believe that they are powerless to change things and determine their own life goals.

In many classrooms today the goal for children is to "get done." They receive so many worksheets and assignments, that merely completing their work is a challenge. How different this "hurry up curriculum" is from that in other countries, where children are expected to do high quality work and are given the time and encouragement to stick with assignments until they are well done. On the walls of schools in England, for example, are writings and artwork with elaborate framing—pieces that obviously took the authors and artists a great deal of time to complete. The work ethic requires perseverance, patience, and diligence, traits that need to be encouraged in the classroom. Children need to accept responsibility for much of their own learning. When teachers set high, but reasonable expectations and encourage hard effort, students learn to be more responsible and diligent.

In children's books there are quite a few examples of persistent, diligent, patient behavior. Reading stories, biographies, and informational books about individuals who have not given up, but persisted in spite of difficult odds is inspiring for children. They learn that hard work has its rewards.

CLASSROOM VIGNETTE

Missy Walsh-Smith, a fourth grade teacher, points out to her students that diligence and perseverance have a long history as traditional American traits, and that in recent years the changing values of our modern culture have tended to obscure their importance in people's minds. Without them, she explains, our society will be reduced to depending on the productivity of other people who are willing to persevere in the face of difficulty. She then shares two very different books with the children so that they can understand that it is never too early to learn these traits.

Eleanor Coerr's *Sadako and the Thousand Paper Cranes* (Illus. by Ronald Himler, Putnam, 1977) is the story of a young girl who lived through the bombing of Hiroshima only to develop leukemia. Sadako becomes a model of hope and perseverance in life, no matter how difficult it is. To encourage her, friends make origami paper cranes . . . 1,000 of them . . . to wish her well and good luck.

After reading the story, Missy asks children to volunteer difficulties they have had in their lives and ways in which they were able, or not able, to overcome obstacles. Sadako's inner strength is discussed and children consider ways in which they can also grow in this dimension. The children make paper cranes to place around the room as reminders of Sadako's perseverance and inspiration for their own.

This book is followed by a more lighthearted one, *Fortunately*, by Remy Charlip (Four Winds, 1964). It is a repetitive picture book designed for younger children, but Missy finds that her fourth graders love it. The book outlines fortunate and unfortunate incidents in the life of the protagonist, who manages to keep a sense of humor while persevering. Missy's fourth graders enjoy choral reading and pantomiming the story. They write their own "fortunately and unfortunately" stories and even news bulletins that tell what has been happening fortunately and unfortunately in the fourth grade classroom.

In Missy's fourth grade class, children refer to these books off and on throughout the year, whenever a renewed focus on diligence and perseverance is needed.

BOOK REVIEWS AND CURRICULAR EXTENSIONS

In the following bibliography, the grade-level designation "P" means the book might be more valuable for the primary grades, kindergarten to grade 3. The designation "I" means the intermediate grades 3-5.

Aardema, Verna. (1981). *Bringing the Rain to Kapiti Plain*. Illus. by Beatriz Vidal. Dial. P, 32 pages.

In a rhyming, cumulative text this African folktale tells about how Ki-pat, a shepherd boy, and his cows endured a drought one year when the rains came late to Kapiti Plain.

Children who have waited patiently for something to happen will relate to this story. In rainy seasons children sometimes wait for the sun to come out so that they can enjoy an outdoor activity. If they live on farms, children know the importance of rain and can relate directly to Ki-pat's predicament. Children might enjoy telling their "waiting" stories and share how they made the time go faster while being patient.

Anderson, Joan. (1991). *Christopher Columbus: From Vision to Voyage.* Illus. by George Ancona. Dial. I, 48 pages.

This biography shares the inner character of Columbus who challenged the narrow-minded thinking of his contemporaries and convinced his supporters that he had the fortitude to endure a dangerous adventure. The illustrations are photographs of Spanish actors and actresses dressed in period costumes.

This book is reminiscent of Walter Piper's *The Little Engine that Could,* Children might talk and write about challenges they have faced and how an optimistic attitude supported their accomplishments. As with so many biographies of Columbus, this one looks only at the man himself, and not at other perspectives of his discovery, such as the impact it had upon the Native Americans and those with problems on shipboard. Role-playing different perspectives of this event might give children the concept that hard work must be accompanied by other ethical qualities for one to be really heroic.

Birdseye, Tom. (1991). *Waiting for Baby.* Illus. by Loreen Leedy. Holiday. P, 32 pages.

A little boy dreams about all the things he will do with the new baby, but when it finally arrives, it is much smaller than the baby he imagined.

Tom Birdseye tells that he wrote this story because his own child was so curious about what their new baby would be like and so eager for the birth to occur. Waiting for a baby is something many children have experienced and can write and tell about. They can also share the ways they have helped care for a new infant sibling.

Burleigh, Robert. (1991). *Flight.* Illus. by Mike Wimmer. Philomel. P, I, 32 pages.

This picture book biography of Charles Lindbergh chronicles his 33-hour flight across the Atlantic Ocean in 1927. It is an extraordinary story of loneliness, fear, courage, and endurance.

Children can discuss their dreams for the future and how difficult those dreams would be to achieve. Virtually all explorers and inventors adventured into the unknown and faced challenges beyond normal daily life occurrences. The challenges faced by these individuals can be charted and compared.

Carle, Eric. (1970). *Pancakes, Pancakes.* Knopf. P, 32 pages.

A boy named Jack follows his mother's directions for every detail of assembling the ingredients for pancakes. He cuts the wheat and takes it to the miller who grinds it into grain, gathers an egg from the hen, milks the cow, churns the butter, and makes the pancakes before he enjoys eating them.

It is hard work to make pancakes, especially the way Jack has to operate. Children can recall times when they helped cook or worked hard on something and the wonderful rewards of completing the task.

Carle, Eric. (1989). *The Very Busy Spider.* Putnam. P, 32 pages.

In *The Very Busy Spider* a spider is too busy spinning her web to play when all her animal friends suggest a frolic. When she finally finishes, there are no rewards for being done except the inner satisfaction that comes from having done a good job. The spider is too tired to even reply to the owl who asks whose fine web it is.

Adults can refer to these books informally as children complete arduous but rewarding projects: "Do you feel like the Very Busy Spider today?" Making a museum or bulletin board to display truly exceptional work helps children celebrate things they worked hard to accomplish. When sharing this book with children, it is important to point out that spiders rarely build their webs at night so that you do not unwittingly pass on information that is not scientifically true.

Carle, Eric. (1990). *The Very Quiet Cricket.* Philomel. P, 32 pages.

A cricket hatches from an egg and tries repeatedly to rub its wings to communicate with other animals, but cannot. Finally, at the end of the book, after much persistence, it makes a cricket sound.

Children face many challenges as they grow up that require repeated efforts to accomplish—tying a shoe, riding a bike, skating, whistling—and in each one the lesson of perseverance can be learned. As children try hard to acquire a new skill, you can refer back to the persistent cricket that tried and tried and tried until it finally succeeded in making a cricket sound.

Children can talk and write about things they have tried and tried to do: riding a bike, roller skating, tying shoe laces, whistling, snapping fingers, and so forth. You might make charts for a bulletin board, such as "I can tie my shoes!" or "I can write my name!" as a way of celebrating those tasks that children worked hard to accomplish. One kindergarten teacher bound a book with each child's name on one page, and his or her picture on the back so that children could correct themselves as they tried to read the names. On the last page was a place for children to sign their names when they could successfully read everyone's name in the book.

Domanska, Janina. (1985). *Busy Monday Morning.* Greenwillow. P, 32 pages.

This song is a chant sung by Polish farmers as they toiled in the fields making hay. In this version, a girl and her father mow, rake, dry, pitch, stack, and haul the hay on each successive day of the week. On Sunday, the last day of the song, they rest together after their week of hard work.

Children can talk about how they work with their parents around the house to mow the lawn, rake leaves, vacuum, or do other chores that are hard work and how pleasant it feels to rest when they are done. They might even compose work chants to sing while they are completing routine tasks.

Freschet, Bernice. (1977). *Elephant & Friends.* Illus. by Glen Rounds. Charles Scribner's. P, I, 32 pages.

All of the animals are tired and hungry because of a serious drought. Elephant decides that something must be done and together the animals embark upon a journey to the other side of the desert where there is a forest. The trek is a real challenge for every one of the animals, but they take turns helping and encouraging each other and even outwit some hunters until, at last, they reach the forest!

Children can recall the patience and perseverance needed on trips they have taken with their families. The class might plan for a long hike or children can recall hikes they have taken in the past and how challenging they are when one becomes tired and thirsty. The idea of cooperating could be highlighted by dividing up what needs to be carried on a hike.

George, Jean Craighead. (1983). *The Talking Earth.* Harper. I, 204 pages.

Billie Wind, a Seminole Indian girl, doubts the legends of her ancestors about talking animals and earth spirits. Billie Wind is sent as punishment into the Everglades alone in a canoe to discover the truth of the Indian lore. The 12-year-old encounters a forest fire, wild animals, and a hurricane; yet successfully provides food and shelter. She befriends an otter, a panther cub, and a turtle, and learns an enormous amount about the interconnections among living things on earth during the several months that she lives in the Everglades alone.

Any adventure story is a story of perseverance. Children might list all the obstacles this girl had to overcome in her quest. In a similar fashion, they could list all the obstacles they have had to overcome in accomplishing a difficult task.

Hall, Donald. (1979). *Oxcart Man.* Illus. by Barbara Cooney. Penguin. P, I, 32 pages.

In this Caldecott award book, a man and his family work hard all year long to raise produce and make items to sell at Portsmouth Market so he can purchase what the family needs for the coming year. The father's long trek to market and back is pictured in illustrations that spread horizontally across the pages, adding to the feeling that the father is on a very long journey.

Children can recall times when their families have worked together for the good of the family. They can share homemade items that they and their families make. Children who can do crafts can teach the others. After they have made some different crafts, the class can sponsor a craft fair or participate in a community fair, selling what they have made. Sometimes classes work together on ways to make money for projects they want to do in school. Children can bake things for a bake sale, donate toys and books they have outgrown, and make a list of similar ways they can make money to meet their needs.

Houston, Gloria. (1988). *The Year of the Perfect Christmas Tree.* Dial. P, I, 32 pages.

It is the turn of Ruthie's family to provide the town's Christmas tree for the local church's pageant on Christmas Eve. Before he goes away to war, Father ties a ribbon on a spruce atop a huge cliff to mark the tree they will cut down for the festivities. Ruthie and her Mother wait and wait for her father's return. When he doesn't make it home by Christmas Eve, they set out together to cut down the tree and her mother makes Ruthie's angel costume for the pageant out of her wedding dress. Set in Appalachia, the story, which is based upon a family experience of Gloria Houston's grandmother, has a very happy ending when Father returns from the war on Christmas Day. The patience exhibited by Ruthie and her mother, and then their hard effort to get the tree down from the hilltop at night, make the father's return very poignant.

Children can recall when they have waited for a family member who has been gone or when they have waited until a holiday to visit a family member. They can talk and write about their family traditions at holiday times and how hard it is to wait each year until the holidays arrive.

Hutchins, Pat. (1990). *What Game Shall We Play?* Greenwillow. P, 32 pages.

A duck and a frog search everywhere for a friend. They ask each animal they encounter the question, "What game shall we play?" They don't give up in their search for a friend. Finally, an owl suggests playing hide-and-go-seek, and all the animals join in for the game.

Children can talk about how they find friends. Discussions can focus on the occasional need to try things over and over before they work and the importance of not giving up. They might write about times when they wanted to give up, but didn't, and what happened as a result.

Ikeda, Daisaku. (1991). *The Snow Country Prince.* Translated by Geraldine McCaughrean. Illus. by Brian Wildsmith. Knopf. P, I, 32 pages.

When the Snow Country Prince visits Mariko and Kazuo to thank them for caring for some wild swans, he tells them, "Whatever happens, don't give up." The children learn why as they nurse an injured bird to health.

Many children have cared for injured animals and know how patient one has to be with them. Have the children tell or write about their own experiences with "not giving up" on animals.

Isadora, Rachel. (1991). *At the Crossroads.* Greenwillow. P, I, 32 pages.

Black South African children are rejoicing over their fathers' return from 10 months in the mines. They make musical instruments to accompany their chants, while they wait patiently at the crossroads all day and all night for the truck that will bring their father home. This book shares the difficult culture of segregated African townships and the very challenging lives lived by the families of men who work in the mines, as well as showing very patient behavior on the part of the children.

Many families have reunions that children await expectantly and can remember long afterwards. Children can talk about separations in their families, when parents have been gone or about joyous family gatherings. They can remember times when they have had to wait patiently for what seemed a very long time for something wonderful to take place.

Keats, Ezra Jack. (1964). *Whistle for Willie.* Penguin. P, 32 pages.

Peter wants to whistle in the worst way. He sees another child whistle and his dog responds immediately. Peter tries and tries to whistle. Finally, when the need is great, he lets out a big whistle, and his dog, Willie, comes directly to him.

Many children enjoy whistling and remember how hard it was to make that first whistle come out. Other children can't do it yet, thus providing an opportunity for the first group to help the second. Both may learn something about diligence and perseverance!

Kellogg, Steven. (1971). *Can I Keep Him?* Dial. P, 32 pages.

A little boy is lonely, so he finds all sorts of animals and tries to convince his mother that he should be able to keep them. She always has an excuse for why he can't. In the end, he finds a friend.

This book and Tony Ross's *I Want a Cat* are similar because the children in them badger their parents for a pet. In *I Want a Cat* the parents give in, while in *Can I Keep Him?* the parent does not. Children can talk about how much they want a pet and what kinds of pets would be best suited to their home and classroom. They can discuss the strategies they use to get their parents to give in and provide them with something they desperately want.

Kherdian, David. (1991). *The Great Fishing Contest.* Illus. by Nonny Hogrogian. Philomel. P, I, 48 pages.

Sammy and Jason, two best friends, plot how they will win the great fishing contest in this short chapter book. There are wonderful examples of true friendship, such as their vow that if one wins the prize (a spinning outfit), both will save an equal amount of money to purchase an identical complete spinning outfit. The boys explore every detail of the pond in which they will be fishing to determine their strategy for the big event. As the white flag waves to end the fishing contest, Jason has just pulled a 10-inch fish from the pond.

Many children enjoy fishing and have experienced the patience needed to catch one. Children can remember the times they had to be patient for things to happen: their cat to have kittens, a new baby to come, a car trip to come to an end, etc. Often patience has its reward, and that can be discussed as well. The class might plan a party or outing for some time in the distance which should provide lessons in patience as well as opportunities to plan the event.

Kroll, Steven. (1988). *Looking for Daniela.* Illus. by Anita Lobel. Holiday. P, I, 32 pages.

Antonio, an acrobat and juggler, enjoys receiving a wave from Daniela prior to his performances. This daughter of a rich merchant slips away and dances with Antonio in the Piazza. One day she is missing! Antonio rescues her and together they travel around the country a step ahead of the bandits.

This story of escaping evil demonstrates the values of strong friendship. Children might talk about how they have helped their friends or their friends have helped them escape a classroom bully or a negative experience.

Levine, Arthur. (1991). *All the Lights in the Night.* Illus. by James Ransome. Tambourine/Morrow. P, I, 32 pages.

Two Jewish boys embark upon a dangerous journey to freedom, escaping Russia. They keep their spirits by telling each other the ancient story of Hanukkah.

Children can recall when storytelling helped remove their fears or when they were on a long and difficult journey.

Lowry, Lois. (1986). *Anastasia Has the Answers.* Houghton Mifflin. I, 130 pages.

Anastasia, a seventh grader, is embarrassed by her inability to climb the ropes in PE class at school. She greatly admires her gym teacher and would do anything to please her. When some international visitors are scheduled to visit the school, Anastasia is given the task of blowing the whistle for the rope climbing demonstration so she will not have to embarrass herself in front of the guests. But the night before, Anastasia rigs up a rope in her garage and practices and practices and practices until she masters climbing to the top of the garage. The question is, can she make it to the top of the gymnasium? Her persistence is obvious in this humorously depicted school situation.

Children can recall things that have been difficult for them to learn and are still difficult for them to do. Charting or graphing their responses would make it obvious that everyone has different talents and interests. Children who have mastered some skills might share them with others. Mini-classes on topics such as origami, whittling, calligraphy, and the like would allow children to share their hard-earned talents with each other and to learn new talents from each other.

McKissack, Patricia C. (1989). *Nettie Jo's Friends*. Knopf. P, 32 pages.

When Mama says that Nettie Jo's favorite doll, Annie Mae, can't come to Cousin Willadeen's wedding because she looks all scraggly, Nettie Jo sets out to find a needle to stitch her up a new dress. Her determination to find that needle lasts through her encounters with three animals, each of whom has a problem to solve. Nettie Jo studies on each problem until she finds a solution. She helps Miz Rabbit fix her floppy ears by tieing them up for her. She helps Mr. Fox see in the bright sunlight by giving him her hat. And she helps Panther call out when he has a cold by lending him a horn. But she still does not have the needle she desperately wants. Discouraged, she starts to walk home, but when she arrives the animals come to thank her and present her with the needle she has been seeking.

Most children have experienced the burning desire for something at some time in their lives. They can relate to Nettie Jo's quest. They can also relate to her disappointment in not finding what she sought. They can talk about times in their lives when they were disappointed and what brought them out of their sad feelings. The animals returning to say thank you might be followed up by a discussion on gratitude and how good it makes us feel when people say "thank you."

Piper, Walter. (1930/1954). *The Little Engine that Could*. Illus. by George Hauman and Doris Hauman. Platt and Munk. P, 32 pages.

In this children's classic, a train engine breaks down while carrying toys and food for Christmas to children who live over a mountain. The large and important engines just pass by the stranded train, but a little blue engine says he will try to take the train over the mountain, chanting, "I think I can, I think I can, I think I can."

This book is perfect to show how hard work pays off and that a positive attitude counts even more than strength and power. Children can talk about times in their lives when positive attitudes have helped them complete challenging projects or to do things they were afraid to do, like diving off a diving board, or going to the school office for the first time. You can informally chant, "I think I can, I think I can" when children are trying hard to do something that is difficult for them.

Provensen, Alice & Provensen, Martin. (1983). *A Glorious Flight Across the Channel with Louis Bleriot*. Viking. P, I, 32 pages.

Papa (Louis Bleriot) is determined to build a flying machine that will fly across the English Channel. When he finally makes that glorious flight, after creating many versions of his aeroplane, there is great rejoicing. This story is a beautiful example of an inventor who used great patience and persistence to accomplish his goals.

Children love to make paper airplanes, but rarely do these planes really fly well. They might work hard until they can create some that meet with real success. In discussions, they can recall times when they have had to try over and over again to do something until they have finally accomplished a task. Examples might be learning to ride a bike, to skate, or to play a piece on a musical instrument.

Ross, Tony. (1989). *I Want a Cat.* Farrar, Straus, & Giroux. P, 32 pages.

A girl wants a cat and tries every strategy imaginable to convince her parents to get her one. She dresses like a cat; sits under the table like a cat; and howls outside like a cat. The neighbors tell the parents they should give in and get her a cat, and when they do, the girl starts acting like a dog.

There are two aspects of this book that children will relate to. One is wanting something so much you can hardly stand it. Children can remember times they wanted something badly, and then, after getting it, realized that what they wanted wasn't quite what they expected it would be. The second aspect of the book with which all children have some experience is in wheedling their parents until they get what they want. Children can talk about how they convince their parents to let them do things they want to do. A chart of their strategies might promote discussion of the most and least effective ways of dealing with parents.

Sanders, Scott Russell. (1989). *Aurora Means Dawn.* Bradbury. P, 32 pages.

This book chronicles the difficult journey of a family moving west by wagon to a town named Aurora. Aurora turns out to be nonexistent, but hiding their disappointment, the family pushes onward and settles in a nearby area.

In addition to the persistence needed by early travelers and by people seeking a goal, the book discusses cooperative family behavior and how to handle disappointments. Children can talk and write about the greatest disappointments in their lives, focusing on the effectiveness of their responses. They might compare this book to the many others about travel westward, or talk and write about challenges faced by their family today and in the past.

Schroeder, Alan. (1989). *Ragtime Tumpie.* Joy Street/Little, Brown. P, I, 32 pages.

Beautiful paintings share the life story of Josephine Baker's childhood and how she was inspired to become one of the greatest dancer/entertainers of the ragtime era. Her continual dancing and interest in music propelled her into performance. It was tiring and hard work, but uplifting as well.

This story will inspire children to identify things they really love to do and to project into the future the impact of those things upon their lives. They can write a possible career book which combines their desires with factual information they have sought from nonfiction sources.

Sis, Peter. (1991). *Follow the Dream: The Story of Christopher Columbus.* Knopf. P, I, 32 pages.

1991 was the year for publication of biographies about Christopher Columbus because of the celebration in 1992 of the 500th anniversary of his voyage across the Atlantic. Any biography of Columbus is bound to emphasize his dedication to the idea of finding the East by sailing west, and his determination to reach land during difficult times at sea. It took Columbus three audiences with King Ferdinand and Queen Isabela to obtain the support he needed for the voyage. Six years after first asking permission, Columbus was finally granted three ships and a crew of 90 men. This particular biography is intricately illustrated with historical documents using a technique resembling fresco painting. Although there are many negative aspects of Columbus' life that are either omitted or glossed over in his biographies (for example, the unnecessary murder of thousands of Native Americans), and it is important to expose children to accurate and complete information, the moral ethic of diligence and perseverance undoubtedly contributed to his success.

Columbus is only one of many explorers who were brave and persistent in meeting the challenges necessary for success. Children might read about other successful explorers or inventors for whom diligence, perseverance, and patience were necessary ingredients for success.

Thiele, Colin. (1991). *Rotten Egg Paterson to the Rescue.* Illus. by Karen Ritz. Harper. I, 144 pages.

Danny rescues an emu egg from the jaws of a hungry lizard and stoically persists in trying to keep the egg safe so that it will hatch. In spite of resistance from his parents, a school bully, and the forces of nature, Danny persists with great determination to save that egg.

Children can talk about times they have persisted in spite of the resistance of others and especially how they have handled the class bully. Many children have tried to save the life of a wild animal in trouble, such as a bird the cat caught or a bird that flew into a window or down the chimney. They can talk and write about these experiences.

Turkle, Brinton. (1978). *Rachel and Obadiah.* Dutton. P, 32 pages.

In the Quaker community on Nantucket Island, the biggest celebration of the year occurs when a ship that has been out at sea returns to harbor. Mr. Slade at the mill is typically the first person to sight the returning ship. He tells a child, who runs to the captain's house to inform the captain's wife. Because Rachel wants to carry the message, she has to beat her bigger brother at a foot race. She perseveres in spite of running in a skirt and falling down. Her efforts are rewarded, as a ship does appear and she becomes the first girl to take the news to the captain's wife.

Children can talk about and write about times when they did not give up, even when the going was tough. Children who swim or run track know what it feels like to be so tired that you don't think you can move another muscle, yet you keep on going. The class could list on a chart all of the inventions or things that would not have happened if the people completing them had quit. It is good to have some long-term ongoing projects in the classroom, like a mural being painted, a quilt being sewn, weaving, or some other craft that children can work on from time to time until it is completed. Another idea is for children to keep a personal record of something they are trying to improve in physical education such as their times for running 100 yards. They could get their times in PE class and record them in their home classrooms.

Williams, Karen Lynn. (1990). *Galimoto.* Illus. by Catherine Stock. Lothrop, Lee & Shepard. P, 32 pages.

Kondi sets his sights on making a galimoto (a wire push toy) even though at first he has very little wire. He trades some of his most prized possessions for wire, and, in time, achieves his goal.

In addition to the insights this story provides into the Malawi culture and the value of homemade toys, this child's persistence in working to solve the challenges of acquiring what he needs is a marvelous example for children here in the United States. The child is only seven and thought by his older brother to be way too young to collect enough wire to make the toy. Two issues could be raised for discussion: (1) what have you ever wanted and worked very hard to accomplish? and (2) what have people told you that you were too young to accomplish? Children could be encouraged to set high, but realistic goals and work for them. The younger the children, the more short-term the goals should be. A class might collect natural materials or recycled materials and explore creatively all that could be made out of their materials, perhaps making homemade toys for younger children. A book link would be with *Captain Snap and the Children of Vinegar Lane* by Roni Schotter (see Chapter 9), because Captain Snap was obviously a diligent collector of junk, which he turns into a museum of homemade crafts.

Winter, Jeanette (1988). *Follow the Drinking Gourd.* Knopf. P, I, 32 pages.

This is the story of a legendary conductor on the Underground Railroad, a one-legged sailor named Peg Leg Joe, who taught slaves the road to freedom by singing a song on how to follow the drinking gourd (the Big Dipper) to the north. The song is interspersed between the story of one family's escape.

This example of extraordinary courage and perseverance can provide a springboard for discussion about heroes who withstood such hardships for the good of humanity. The hero inside each of us might be explored. What in our lives is really worth extraordinary efforts?

Yashima, Taro. (1955). *Crow Boy.* Viking. P, I, 32 pages.

A rural Japanese boy walks a long distance to school every day for six years. The schoolchildren make fun of him and call him Chibi until, in the sixth grade, a sensitive teacher, Mr. Isobe, recognizes his talents. For the school talent show, Chibi imitates the many calls of crows he has heard on his long walk to and from school, and is thus remembered by all of the townspeople as Crow Boy. This poor boy with no friends is the only student in the school with perfect attendance for all six years, in spite of the fact that he had the farthest to walk to school.

Children can keep records over a long term on their behaviors, such as how many days in a row they can make their beds without being asked, or practice the piano, or remember to bring their lunches to school. Charts can be constructed to record school attendance and tardiness. Children might talk about how much harder it is to be persistent when you are different from the others (see Chapter 9 for book links on this topic). They can be encouraged to write of personal experiences in which they felt, even a little, like Crow Boy.

SUMMARY

The books in this chapter range from nonfiction biographies (*Follow the Dream, Ragtime Tumpie,* and *A Glorious Flight*) and historical fiction (*The Year of the Perfect Christmas Tree, Aurora Means Dawn, Oxcart Man, The Glorious Flight, All the Lights in the Night,* and *Follow the Drinking*

Gourd) to fictional stories and a song. A wide range of ethnic diversity is represented in these books. They take place in Africa, Japan, Appalachia, South Africa, France, and Egypt. In addition to these cultures, *Rachel and Obadiah* depicts a Quaker family, *Nettie Jo's Friends* is a southern folktale, and *Busy Monday Morning* is a Polish chant. Multicultural diversity in books shows children that the values and morals represented are universal ones. Historically, it is the people who have been diligent, persistent, and hard working who have succeeded when other less resourceful people have not.

It is interesting to record the issues or life experiences that have prompted people's diligence in story books. Explorers and inventors (as in *Flight, The Glorious Flight,* and *Follow the Dream*) must persevere. Likewise, people on a quest or adventure often have challenges to overcome as they pursue their goal. The goal is freedom in *Follow the Drinking Gourd,* a new home in the West in *Aurora Means Dawn,* kinship to the earth and survival in *The Talking Earth* and *Looking for Daniela,* a friend in *What Game Shall We Play,* and a needle in *Nettie Jo's Friends.*

People must be persistent when learning a new skill or trying to do something that is difficult for them. *The Very Quiet Cricket* wants to make a cricket sound; Peter wanted to whistle in *Whistle for Willie*; Anastasia wants to climb the ropes to the gymnasium ceiling in *Anastasia Has the Answers*; the little engine wants to make it over the mountain in *The Little Engine that Could*; and Rachel wants to win the race in *Rachel and Obadiah.* Daily chores and routine experiences can provide challenges as well, often followed by rest and relaxation. The spider must avoid interruptions while spinning a web in *The Very Busy Spider* and falls asleep when the web is completed. Each day something different must be done to the hay in *Busy Monday Morning* until at last on Sunday the child and father can rest together. A father walks all the way to Portsmouth Harbor and home again in *Oxcart Man* and his family works all year to provide the goods for him to sell. Jack works very hard to make his pancake breakfast in *Pancakes, Pancakes!* And Chibi walks to school every day for six years from his distant home in the country in *Crow Boy.* Sometimes our diligence is required in spite of the opposition of others, as when Danny saves an emu egg from a lizard and cares for it until it hatches in *Rotten Egg Paterson to the Rescue.*

Waiting can require a great deal of patience. A child in *Waiting for Baby* waits for his baby brother or sister to be born. The children in *The Snow Country Prince* must wait for a swan to heal. The children in *At the Crossroads* wait patiently for their fathers to return from the mines. Fishing requires patience in *The Great Fishing Contest.* Ki-pat had to wait for the rains in *Bringing the Rain to Kapiti Plain.* Children must wait for the pet they so desperately want in *I Want a Cat* and *Can I Keep Him?* And Kondi must wait until he acquires enough wire to begin making his push toy in *Galimoto*.

It is the difficult times we have endured and grown from which make their marks on our lives and are what we write and tell stories about. The same is true for children, which is why telling and writing stories is such a natural book extension activity for this topic in literature. Setting goals and then trying to meet them, charting and graphing progress, and recording in writing our accomplishments all link well with this topic of study.

CHAPTER 12

Unconditional Love

RATIONALE

In moral development theory, the highest level that any human can attain is to express unconditional love. A few people attain this state on a long-term basis and, if they do so publicly, are almost ensured a place in history. Jesus Christ and Mahatma Gandhi are often cited as examples. Many other people can and do express this wonderful attitude at various times in their lives. Perhaps there are people you know who are unconditionally loving, although they will not make the history books.

It takes a certain amount of maturity to achieve this state and, therefore, we can't expect to see more than a glimpse of it in children. But it is never too soon to begin fostering such love and to help children recognize and appreciate it when it is expressed toward them. Within the classroom, teachers can comment informally when they see love expressed. (In the upper grades it may be wise not to call it love, directly, because of children's changing definitions of the word.) Teachers model unconditional love when they separate children's inappropriate actions from the children themselves. When they say, "In this classroom hitting is not allowed," they are on the way toward showing a child that, although the action will not be tolerated, the child is still loved.

The competition that is fostered in most schools works against the development of unconditional love and in the direction of jealousy and self-interest. When students compete for grades, for the teacher's attention, for limited resources and the attention of their peers, they think only of their own survival. When teachers promote cooperative learning, and couple that with appropriate encouraging comments about loving behavior, growth in the right direction is more likely to take place.

Components of unconditional love can be seen in even very young children. Every time children are loving, caring, or considerate with no expectation of a reward or consequence, they are loving unconditionally. When children help someone out, not because they are asked to or because there is something in it for them, they are making choices based upon their own internal reasoning rather than an extrinsic reinforcer. They are responding to a need of someone else instead of their own needs and desires.

For the purposes of this chapter, we are defining unconditional love as love or caring provided for someone else when there is no expectation of a reward. The idea is to foster doing good and being loving just because those behaviors make us feel good inside. So often children are loving and kind, but only because there is a payoff. In these cases, the only payoff is in helping someone else or loving someone else without other conditions present. (Unlike the chapter on respecting and appreciating others, this chapter focuses upon caring for others who are close to us or providing for the needy. That chapter also contains books where caring behaviors are seen, but those behaviors are for people who are different in some striking way from the person providing the care.)

There are many opportunities in school for giving comfort and aid to others. Children learn to be encouraging of others when that kind of behavior is modeled by the adults in the classroom. A caring classroom invites children to cooperate and help others continually. Children can reach out to those in need in very tangible ways. One second grade prepared a meal for a family whose mother was coming home from the hospital. The children planned the menu, did the shopping, and cooked a variety of dishes. The teacher videotaped some of the activity for the mother to watch at home. Another class used a web to brainstorm all the possible ways the class could participate in helping the less fortunate during the winter holidays. The class ended up adopting a family for Thanksgiving dinner and participating in a Christmas gift sharing program. Reaching out to the less fortunate helps children feel worthwhile, needed, and responsible.

It is important for the curriculum to include many opportunities for children to see and hear about people who demonstrate kindness, self-sacrifice, and consideration of one another. Children's literature includes quite a few models of this kind of love. In the books reviewed in this chapter there are people who are kind and caring to others with no thought of benefit to themselves. When stories like these are shared with children, they learn that it can be natural to be thoughtful and helpful when the need arises. They begin to learn that, although sometimes difficult, it is possible to love others—all others—no matter what.

CLASSROOM VIGNETTE

Some books appeal to people of all ages. *Love You Forever* by Robert Munsch (Illus. by Shiela McGraw, Firefly, 1986) is such a book. It can bring everyone from kindergartners to senior citizens to tears because it touches the heart of everyone, since we all have mothers who have loved us unconditionally. Kathy found that the book broadened kindergarten children's understanding of the term love and showed them a variety of ways to express love.

This story follows a newborn baby through life as a toddler, little boy, adolescent, and finally an adult father who cares for his dependent mother. In delightfully humorous vignettes we see the boy flushing the mother's wristwatch down the drain as a toddler, singing as a teenage rock star, and moving across town to live. The message is clear, that whatever the child does, his mother will always love him. The refrain at each stage in life is sung by the mother as she rocks her child, and later her son who has become a grown man: "I'll love you forever, I'll like you for always, As long as I'm living my baby you'll be." The child, when grown at the end of the story, sings the same chant to his mother, telling her that, "As long as I'm living my Mommy you'll be." In spite of all the horrid, strange things the child has done, his mother unconditionally loves him, and he returns that love.

Kathy wrote the words to the refrain on chart paper and read the story to a kindergarten class, having them sing the refrain along with her. She then asked them to help her make a chart on "How do your parents show that they love you?" The children gave her responses like: "By a hug," "They tuck me into bed at night," "They buy me stuff," and "They read to me." She then asked, "How do you show your parents that you love them?" Typical responses included: "With a hug," "By helping out at home," "Setting the table," "Feeding the dog," and "Picking up my toys." This book provided a wonderful opportunity for children to learn that there are many ways to give unconditional love. Through an appreciation of the diversity of the ways to give love, children are able to develop an understanding that there are abundant ways to share love with others.

BOOK REVIEWS AND CURRICULAR EXTENSIONS

In the following bibliography, the grade-level designation "P" means the book might be more valuable for the primary grades, kindergarten to grade 3. The designation "I" means the intermediate grades 3-5.

Bang, Molly. (1985). *The Paper Crane.* Greenwillow. P, I, 32 pages.

A hardworking man runs a very successful restaurant until a new highway is built close by and travelers no longer stop at his establishment. One evening a stranger, wearing old, worn clothes, enters and admits he has no money to pay for food. The owner makes him the best meal he can make and serves him like a king. The stranger thanks him with a paper crane that will become a living bird and dance when the owner of the restaurant claps his hands. This crane attracts many more people to the restaurant.

There are two ways children might relate to this book. One is to have them research how hungry people are cared for in their own community and perhaps organize a way to support that effort. The other is for children to remember when they did something for someone in need or without money. Older children can focus discussion of the book and their own follow-up activities on the love that is expressed without thought of reward.

Beck, Martine. (1991). *The Rescue of Brown Bear and White Bear.* Illus. by Marie H. Henry. Little, Brown. P, I, 32 pages.

When an avalanche destroys the home of Brown Bear and White Bear just before the arrival of their baby, a group of bears from town comes with ladders and saws, hammers and nails, to help out just in the nick of time.

　　Emergencies often spark helpful and caring behaviors. Children may be able to recall times when their family had a problem and they had to help out in unusual ways. You can review the procedures to follow during an emergency at home or at school. Children might suggest ways they could be helpful to a family that is expecting a baby.

Christian, Peggy. (1991). *The Old Coot.* Illus. by Eileen Christelow. Atheneum. I, 64 pages.

The Old Coot only comes down out of the mountain twice a year for supplies and is very antisocial. One day a coyote tells him that he will show the Old Coot a river of gold in exchange for some food. The Old Coot agrees and travels for weeks with the coyote, not realizing that the river of gold is the many stories he tells the coyote during their travels. From then on the old coot shares his stories with the world in exchange for food or in storytelling contests, which keep alive the history and culture of the Old West.

　　Here is an example of a lonely person having a great deal to offer if that person is approached in the right way. There are many individuals in any community with stories to tell. In this case, it is a coyote that taps the treasure, but in a classroom children might talk about how they might discover storytellers in their own community and through oral histories write and publish stories about their hometown.

Cutting, Michael. (1991). *The Little Crooked Christmas Tree.* Illus. by Ron Broda. Scholastic. P, I, 24 pages.

A little evergreen tree responds to the request of a stranded white dove to provide shelter for it during a snowstorm. By crooking its branches, the tree gives the bird a safe refuge from the storm. But this act of kindness makes the little tree unsuitable as a Christmas tree. After a season of rejection, it is planted in a family's yard and again ignored until the Christmas season rolls around once again, when the family transforms the tree into a spectacular outdoor decoration.

　　Children can talk about feelings of rejection and about how their loving behaviors have returned love to them in unexpected ways. Holiday times tend to bring out love in wonderful ways which can be shared in writing and remembered.

dePaola, Tomie. (1974). *Watch Out for the Chicken Feet in Your Soup.* Prentice-Hall. P, 32 pages.

An embarrassed Joey brings his friend Eugene to visit his grandma. Joey's feelings turn to jealousy when he sees the lavish attention his friend receives from his grandma. But his jealousy subsides when the boys leave and Joey gets the largest bread doll and his grandma tells why: "Because you are my special Joey."

This Italian grandma goes way out of her way to make the boys feel loved and to include Joey's friend in the family routines. Children can recall experiences they have had with other families or when their family has included one of their friends for an activity.

Fox, Mem. (1989). *Koala Lou.* Harcourt Brace Jovanovich. P, 32 pages.

"Koala Lou, I do love you," sings her mother repeatedly. But as new baby brothers and sisters enter the family, Koala Lou hears these words less frequently and decides to earn her mother's affections by winning the gum tree climbing event in the Koala Olympics. After days of hard practice, the time finally comes, and Koala Lou does not win, but comes in second. She cries her eyes out and hides until evening when she finally returns home. Her mother throws her arms around her and sings, "Koala Lou, I do love you!" Her mother's love is not conditional upon winning contests.

Children today who come from busy families where parents forget or neglect to say "I love you," need reassurance that, no matter what happens, their parents will always love them. Since many young people today participate, even from early ages, in competitive sports and musical events, discussions about what is important on such occasions will be helpful. It is not winning that counts, but trying and doing your best. This can be a hard lesson for children to learn.

Greenfield, Eloise. (1988). *Grandpa's Face.* Putnam. P, 32 pages.

A little girl becomes terrified when she sees her grandfather practicing for his role in a theatrical production by putting on a very nasty face. She's never seen anything but his loving face. He assures her that he will always love her and never let her see the hateful face again.

Many grandparents typically give children their unconditional love. Children can talk about and write about the things they like to do with their grandparents and how they feel their grandparents' love. They can talk about frightening experiences they have had and how a parent or grandparent has consoled them. They can talk about faces and how they feel when they see a smiling face, an angry face, a sneering face, etc. This might be tied into an art lesson on drawing or making paper bag masks of such faces.

Harshman, Marc. (1990). *Snow Country.* Illus. by Leslie W. Bowman. Cobblehill/ Dutton. P, 32 pages.

When the worst snowstorm in 20 years hits, Teddy's mom takes in a string of neighbors who are stranded by the storm even though she and Teddy are worried about his dad not coming home. They all sleep in the living room, telling stories to calm their fears.

Children can relate to the fears they have experienced during severe storms and how they or others have been helpful and loving under such conditions. They can review emergency procedures and think of ways to make experiencing unusual weather more pleasant. For example, they might learn stories to tell, or collect especially good books to store along with food supplies.

Hughes, Shirley. (1988). *Dogger.* Lothrop, Lee & Shepard. P, 32 pages.

When David loses Dogger, his stuffed pet, his whole family pitches in to help him look for it. His big sister, Bella, kindly lends him one of her teddy bears at bedtime, but that is not the same as Dogger. The next day at the carnival, Dogger appears at a used toy stand, but before David can get him back, a little girl buys the stuffed animal. Bella comes to his rescue by trading a huge teddy she has just won for Dogger.

A beautiful counter to the typical sibling rivalries described in picture books, *Dogger* can help children think of ways their big sisters and brothers have cared for them or they have cared for their younger siblings. Children might discuss the responsibilities of having siblings and their roles in promoting a caring relationship with their siblings.

Joosse, Barbara. (1988). *Better with Two*. Illus. by Catherine Stock. Harper & Row. P, 32 pages.

Each morning Laura accompanies Mrs. Brady and her old dog, Max, on a walk and for "elevenses" (or tea). When Max dies, Laura cries. Her Mama hugs her until she's finished. "Crying is better with two," Mama says. Mrs. Brady still sits on her bench swing, but without Max, it rocks crooked. Mrs. Brady looks lonely and very sad. Laura gives Mrs. Brady a china dog like Max, some flowers, a drawing, and finally sits with her on her swing and takes tea to Mrs. Brady in a paper bag. This reinstates their former routine of having tea at eleven, and Mrs. Brady realizes that she can be happy without her old friend.

This book is about meeting the needs of someone else and also about love and caring for both animals and friends. It shows children things they can do when people are sad. Children can remember how they were comforted when they were sad. They could make a chart of activities that are "better with two."

Kimmell, Eric. (1989). *Herschel and the Hanukkah Goblins*. Illus. by Trina Schart Hyman. Holiday House. P, I, 32 pages.

Herschel rescues a village from goblins who have terrified the residents into not celebrating their beloved Hanukkah. In this entertaining trickster tale, Herschel outwits the goblins, overcoming their evil spell, thus allowing the townspeople to celebrate their religious holiday once again.

In addition to informing children in an entertaining way about the traditions of the Hanukkah holiday, this tale shows what great dedication and commitment Herschel had to doing good. Discussions might include the occasional need for sacrifice when we do things for other people. To make others happy, we sometimes have to do things we don't want to do. Children might list ways they have helped out in situations when they would have preferred doing other things.

Kroll, Steven. (1988). *Happy Father's Day*. Illus. by Marylin Hafner. Holiday. P, 32 pages.

All seven of his children and their mom do kind and thoughtful things for Dad on Father's Day, such as take out the trash, paint the cellar door, mow the lawn, knit a pair of socks, wash the car, and make him breakfast. It is obvious that he appreciates these caring gifts every bit as much as, if not more than, gifts money can buy.

Children might brainstorm all of the thoughtful gifts of service they could provide for their families and others. In school they might make gift certificates to be cashed in when the services are provided. Or, the classroom might be turned into a gift-making workshop where thoughtful homemade gifts could be produced.

Levitin, Sonia. (1991). *The Man Who Kept His Heart in a Bucket.* Illus. by Jerry Pinkney. Dial. P, I, 32 pages.

Jack's heart had once been broken, so he carried it around in a bucket. Jack is a metal worker who sets out to find work. His customers give him unconditional love—the baker a piece of delicious berry pie, the piper a lively mazurka, and a poor family some vegetables and a chance to hold their baby. But Jack cannot truly enjoy these gifts because he cannot use his heart in the bucket. After Jack takes orders from these people, he stops at a lake to get more water for his heart, but a fish steals his heart and turns into a beautiful maiden. When Jack delivers the pans to the baker, the tin cup to the piper, and the swing for the couple's baby, he discovers that his heart is now in the right place. He makes the maiden a wedding ring, and they celebrate love with the baker, piper, and mother and father.

This is a touching tale about caring for someone who is hurting inside. Younger children will simply enjoy the well-told tale and expressive illustrations. They will notice and talk about what makes Jack happy and how they can make others happy. Older children will see the deeper theme of unrequited love and the healing of a broken heart.

Loh, Morag. (1988). *Tucking Mommy In.* Orchard. P, 32 pages.

While putting her two children to bed and telling them their nighttime story, Mommy falls asleep. The children, who are wide awake, decide they need to tuck Mommy in. They help her get undressed and tell her a story to put her to sleep. Her modeling of gentle bedtime behavior is reflected in the children's caring for her.

Children at school can recall their bedtime routines and write about how they like to go to sleep at night. They can relate how their parents or grandparents take care of them, or the occasions when they have taken care of their parents when the parents were especially sleepy or not feeling well. If they haven't done this before, the discussion could lead there.

Lyon, George Ella. (1990). *Come a Tide.* Illus. by Stephen Gammell. Orchard. P, 32 pages.

Each year when the spring floods come, the families living on the mountain by the river listen to the radio to hear the weather report. When the whistle comes, they know to evacuate because they will be flooded out. Offering help along the way, one family makes it to Grandma's on top of the hill. When the children ask what they should do the next morning, Grandma advises them, "If it was me, I'd make friends with a shovel." They and their neighbors shovel all day eating lunch at the rescue wagon. The horrors of a scary spring flood are counterbalanced by the camaraderie of the neighbors helping each other.

Children who have never experienced a Welcome Wagon, might have experienced people sharing food after a funeral, when they have moved into a new neighborhood, or during some other time of stress in their lives. Some will have shared their lunch with a child who has forgotten lunch money. One second grade class prepared an elaborate meal for the family of one of the children in the class when their mother came home from the hospital. Reaching out to others in emergencies is something that can be demonstrated in school.

Moore, Inga. (1991). *Six-Dinner Sid*. Simon & Schuster. P, I, 32 pages.

Sid, the cat, lives at six different homes and has six different families that take care of him. No one discovers his multiple identities until he is taken to the vet, not once, but six times!

This is a touching and humorous story about how people care for animals while still leaving them their independence. Children will relate stories of how they have fed and found homes for stray animals and about "neighborhood" animals that befriend everyone who gives them attention. Children can talk about how caring for animals is not unlike caring for people.

Morris, Ann. (1990). *Loving*. Lothrop, Lee & Shepard. P, I, 32 pages.

In beautiful color photographs, people from around the world are shown loving each other, demonstrating the universality of affection.

Children can enjoy this book individually or discuss as a group the feelings it elicits and the ways in which its ideas can be applied to their own lives. Children might bring in photographs showing love among their family members to place on a bulletin board on the theme of "Loving."

Palmer, Kate Salley. (1991). *A Gracious Plenty*. Simon & Schuster. P, I, 32 pages.

Great-aunt Mary is a strong, independent woman who lives alone. She has a family who loves her and has dinner with her once a week and many people who miss her when she goes away and are glad when she comes home. Great-aunt appreciates the love she receives from her family and friends and states that she has "a gracious plenty."

There are several moral lessons in this book. One is that a woman can be a strong, independent, single person. So many children's books portray the ideal lifestyle as that of being married and having children. The children might talk about independent single women they know. Another message is that each of us is surrounded by love. Even if one has no children, there is family and there are friends who become like family to us. The children might talk and write about their very special friends who are like family to them. We all need to love and appreciate those around us.

Polacco, Patricia. (1991). *Some Birthday!* Simon & Schuster. P, I, 40 pages.

Patricia, whose parents are divorced, spends the summer with her dad and his mother, her grandmother. One year she thinks the whole family has forgotten her birthday until late in the evening when they play a big trick on her. Her birthday that year turns out to be the scariest, funniest, and best birthday ever.

One of the times when children most realize the unconditional love of their parents is at birthday times. Children will have fun recalling their funniest, best, and most memorable birthday celebrations.

Sendak, Maurice. (1963). *Where the Wild Things Are*. Harper. P, 32 pages.

When Max is naughty he is sent to his bedroom where he imagines a fantasy voyage to where the wild things are. After cavorting with them for a time, he decides to return home, and, when he does, he finds his supper waiting for him. And it is still hot. His mother loves him, even when he has been naughty.

Children can discuss the times when they have been naughty, yet still felt their parents' love. They can recount all the things their parents do for them and express appreciation for their parents. Some children will not have experienced this kind of forgiveness on the part of their parents, which may lead to discussions of ways they wish their parents would treat them.

Spinelli, Eileen. (1991). *Somebody Loves You, Mr. Hatch.* Illus. by Paul Yalowitz. Bradbury. P, I, 32 pages.

Mr. Hatch lives a dull, routinized life working at a shoelace factory, stopping at the newsstand to get the paper and the grocery story to buy a fresh turkey wing for his supper, and then returning home to be by himself. People said, "He keeps to himself." In dull, shaded colors, his life is pictured as being drab and uninteresting, until one day the postman delivers a huge box full of candy for Valentine's Day with a note on it that says, "Somebody loves *you*." Mr. Hatch's life is transformed. He starts talking to people. He volunteers to watch the newsstand so that its proprietor can go to the doctor, shares his candy at work, and purchases ham instead of turkey wings for supper. Everyone is astonished at the "new" Mr. Hatch. Then, the postman returns to announce that the huge Valentine was a mistake; it had been delivered to the wrong address. Mr. Hatch returns to his former sullen self until all his neighbors and new friends greet him with a banner that says, "Everybody Loves Mr. Hatch."

Children can discuss how to help and support people who are very shy, quiet, lonely, sad, or different in other ways. Like the worst person in James Stevenson's *The Worst Person's Christmas*, Mr. Hatch is not a very friendly sort. Holiday times are good times to reach out to people with whom we may not have opportunities for friendly interactions on a daily basis. Children can gather all the ways available to care for other people at holiday times.

Steig, William. (1969). *Sylvester and the Magic Pebble.* Simon & Schuster. P, 32 pages.

Sylvester, a donkey, is turned into a stone by holding a magic pebble and making a wish. His parents are distraught by his disappearance, and search for him diligently for months until, finally, in the spring, they find the pebble, place it on the stone (which is Sylvester), and he comes alive again. This is a marvelous example of parents' love and devotion for their child.

This might be a good book to share prior to Mothers' or Fathers' Day when children need reasons to love and appreciate all the wonderful things their parents do for them.

Stevenson, James. (1991). *The Worst Person's Christmas.* Greenwillow. P, I, 32 pages.

The worst person is at his worst at Christmas, when everyone else is brimming with good cheer. Instead of enjoying Christmas lights, they keep him awake at night and waste electricity. Instead of welcoming carolers, he sits waiting to chase them off his property. Some children wonder why he is so grouchy and set out to change that by giving him a Christmas present. As he takes the present to the garbage can, he falls on their sled, and is propelled into a Christmas party to which he had been invited by a neighbor. The hilarious chain of events ends up turning him into a cheerful person. Written in cartoon format, this funny book will appeal to all ages of children.

Children might think about how to get along with people who are grouchy or sad. Holidays are good times to remember people who might be lonely or sad. This book and Eileen Spinelli's *Someone Loves You, Mr. Hatch* make perfect book links on this topic.

Wallner, John. (1990). *Good King Wenceslas*. Philomel. P, I, 32 pages.

A song in book form with lyrics that tell of a good king who, with his page, goes out into the cold snow to share food with a poor man. The end summarizes the moral of the song: "Therefore, Christian men, be sure, wealth or rank possessing, Ye who now will bless the poor, shall yourselves find blessing." One of the best ways to feel good about ourselves is to help those who are less fortunate.

At the holiday season there are many avenues open for children to donate to worthy causes and help those who are in need. One class began earning money early in the school year, so that by Christmas time they were able to contribute to several worthy causes. Many elementary school classrooms adopt a poor family for the holidays, providing presents and food for the family's holiday. Giving to the less fortunate is a habit which needs to be cultivated in young children; and it is important to do this in a way that is not condescending, but shows respect and unconditional love for all people.

Watson, Wendy. (1991). *A Valentine for You*. Clarion/Houghton Mifflin. P, I, 32 pages.

This collection of traditional love verses, some humorous, some touching, is accompanied by old fashioned illustrations. A delightful collection for Valentine's Day or any day for expressing love to those who are special to us.

Since most of the poems are very simply written, children might write their own witty or touching rhymes to celebrate their love for others. A collection of such rhymes would make a lovely Valentine gift.

Willard, Nancy. (1990). *The High Rise Glorious Skittle Skat Roarious Sky Pie Angel Food Cake*. Illus. by Richard Jesse Watson. Harcourt Brace Jovanovich. P, I, 32 pages.

The wonderful love between a mother and daughter shines throughout this story. In the beginning, the daughter asks her mother what she would like for her birthday. The mother requests a chocolate cake because the daughter likes chocolate—she is thinking of her daughter, even when deciding upon a birthday present for herself. The daughter's love is evident in the rest of the story as she searches everywhere for her grandmother's favorite cake recipe and finally bakes the cake for her mother. This book would also fit nicely into the chapter on perseverance, as the child must persevere to find the recipe and then, again, to make the cake.

The cake is an old family recipe. Children might gather old family recipes to put in a cookbook as a way of sharing their family lore.

Williams, Vera B. (1982). *A Chair for My Mother*. Greenwillow. P, 32 pages.

A special aspect of this book is that it is the child who is expressing unconditional love for her parent. After a devastating house fire, Rosa's family replaces most of what they had, but they lack a comfortable chair. Her mother, who is a waitress, comes home exhausted every night, so the family decides to save money to purchase a stuffed armchair. In a large jar, the mother places the tips she makes on her job, an aunt and uncle contribute, and the child even donates a little change she has earned. When the money jar is full, Rosa and her aunt and uncle purchase that very special chair for her mother.

There are several values expressed here. Strong family love and caring are evident. Saving for something special is an ethic worth appreciating. A class can take on a charitable project and then plan how to save money to support their benevolence.

Williams, Vera B. (1990). *"More More More," Said the Baby: Three Love Stories*. Greenwillow. P, 32 pages.

Three babies with pet names, Little Guy, Little Pumpkin, and Little Bird, are each given close loving attention by a father, a grandmother, and a mother, causing each one to laugh and cry out for, "More, More, More!" The vibrant illustrations depict multi-cultural children and family members in this Caldecott honor book.

The unconditional love and playfulness of the adults in this story might elicit happy memories from children about their own playful experiences with adults in their families. The children might write their own love stories, which would make lovely gifts to those they are remembering. Nicknames often indicate special love and caring relationships, and children may want to research their names or nickname origins and write about them. Children can also write about experiences in their lives that they wish they had more of.

Wittman, Sally. (1982). *The Wonderful Mrs. Trumbly*. Illus. by Margot Apple. Harper. P, 32 pages.

Martin develops a huge crush on Mrs. Trumbly, his second grade teacher. They talk together on the playground; he walks her to her bus stop; he notices every detail about her life. When she starts spending a lot of time with Mr. Klein, the music teacher, Martin becomes very jealous. In the end he learns that Mrs. Trumbly can love and even marry Mr. Klein, but still love Martin as a very special friend as well.

Most children have had crushes on someone older—a teacher, camp counselor, or babysitter to whom they have become unusually close. These special people might be the focus of study, with the children writing stories or biographies about their very special friends.

SUMMARY

The books reviewed in this chapter tend to be sweet stories of human kindness, demonstrating a variety of forms of love. Some deal with the kind of unconditional love that is precipitated by emergencies such as snow-storms (*Snow Country*), floods (*Come a Tide*), an avalanche (*The Rescue of Brown Bear and White Bear*), the death of a pet (*Better with Two*), the appearance of a poor stranger (*The Paper Crane*), the appearance of something very frightening like goblins (*Herschel and the Hanukkah Goblins*), or some other occasion when everyone pulls together to help those who are less fortunate (*Good King Wenceslas*).

The rest of the stories of unconditional love are represented by the special kind of love that families or very good friends share. Grandparents (*Grandpa's Face* and *Watch Out for the Chicken Feet in Your Soup*), families (*A Gracious Plenty*), parents (*Happy Father's Day, More, More, More*), siblings (*Dogger, Air Mail to the Moon*), and good friends (*Pages of Music, The Wonderful Mrs. Trumbly*) are shown to be unusually loving and caring. One occasion when most children receive special love from their families is their birthdays. Patricia thinks everyone has forgotten hers in *Some Birthday!* until she discovers that her family has tricked her into the funniest, most memorable birthday of all.

Two books explore the dual issues of loneliness at holiday times and caring for someone who appears on the surface to be grouchy (*The Worst Person's Christmas* and *Somebody Loves You, Mr. Hatch.*) As explained in *Captain Snap and the Children of Vinegar Lane* (reviewed in Chapter 9) and *The Old Coot*, eccentric people need to experience unconditional love.

When an emergency arises—furniture is lost in a fire (*A Chair for My Mother*), a stuffed animal is lost (*Dogger*), or a child doesn't come in first in a contest (*Koala Lou*)—the family pitches in to solve problems and express unconditional love. Even when a child does something naughty or stupid (*Where the Wild Things Are, Sylvester and the Magic Pebble*), their parents forgive them and express their love. There is only one nonfiction book (*Loving*) and one book of poetry (*A Valentine for You*) included in this chapter; however, there are many books containing love poems that could also support the theme of unconditional love.

Sometimes animals bring forth unconditional love on the part of the people who care for them. Animals have their own unique personalities and often need unconditional love. The cat in *Six-Dinner Sid* cons six different families into feeding and caring for him. Loving behavior is rewarded by loving behavior in another book, *The Little Crooked Christmas Tree*, where after providing a home for a stranded white dove, a tree unsuitable to most as a Christmas tree, receives a family's love at Christmas time.

The follow-up activities are clustered around helping those who are less fortunate and being unusually kind and caring to family members. A class can respond to unforeseen events (sending cards to a child in the hospital, collecting food and clothing for a family hurt by a fire, and expressing sympathy after a death). When linked to children's literature with similar situations, these events can provide children many avenues to experience at their own developmental level aspects of unconditional love. The books with child protagonists who are kind and caring (*Tucking Mommy In*) provide especially good models of this type of behavior in a world where not all children may experience unconditional love first hand.

Index

This index contains authors and titles of books as well as subjects.